AIDING ISLAM

SIMON LENNON

Aiding Islam
Non-fiction
Islam, Terrorism
A book in the collection: The West
A book in the series: Cultures
Published by Pine Hill Books
Copyright © 2016, 2021 by Simon Lennon.
All rights reserved.
This book or any portion thereof may not be reproduced, stored in or introduced into a retrieval system, or transmitted in any form or by any means whatsoever (electronic, mechanical, photocopying, recording, or otherwise) without the express written prior permission of the author and the publisher, except for the use of brief quotations in a book review, scholarly journal, or student assignment.
The author asserts his moral rights.
ISBN 978-1-925446-07-4 (electronic)
ISBN 978-1-925446-21-0 (paperback)
58,000 words, plus bibliography, references to 64,000 words
Cover image: Glenrowan, 2013

In memory of my paternal grandfather

CONTENTS

1. The Age of Ideology 1
2. The Unfinished War 9
3. Multiculturalism at War 16
4. September Eleven, 2001 23
5. Losing their Religion 30
6. Staving off Prejudice 38
7. Abandoning the Vulnerable 46
8. Western Individualism 53
9. The Peace of Nations 60
10. Muslim Nationalism 66
11. Solidarity 73
12. Other Peoples' Rights 80
13. Freedom from Speech 87
14. Integration 96
15. Race 102
16. Religion 109
17. Defending Multiculturalism 116
18. Wartime Propaganda 124
19. Christians 131
20. Islamic Land 139
21. Our Lands of Other People 147
22. Eurabia 155
23. Redefining our Fallen 162
Bibliography, References 168
About the Author 189

1. THE AGE OF IDEOLOGY

My paternal grandfather said little of the Second World War, except to explain his uniform was doused red by the blood of an Australian soldier standing beside him, killed by Japanese. Brave men and women aren't fearless. They're frightened, but do what virtue demands they do. My grandfather was a medical officer on Labuan, who parachuted into Changi Prison, Singapore, in 1945. Japanese guards stood around shocked by their emperor's surrender, without thought of helping the British, Australian, and other prisoners of war they'd worked to near death.

All men aren't created equal. There are no inalienable rights, no universal values. All cultures aren't equal, least of all for people who've suffered because of particular cultures.

For a people who talk so much of the world, the West today is stunningly ignorant of the forces affecting us. Of all the killing throughout the world since Cain killed Abel, the most influential upon our time, still driving Western values, were the two world wars, but not the wars that were. World War II became the war redefined in retrospect: our retrospective war against prejudice, but only white people's prejudice.

The French Revolution from 1789 had sought to replace the old European order with a new European civilisation. Rejecting that revolution for being bourgeois, nineteenth-century Jewish atheist Karl Marx rejected European civilisation altogether. Promising a new world civilisation to those who'd lost faith in Western Civilisation, Marxist communism found its footing through World War I. The Age of Ideology began.

After winning power through revolution and civil war in the ravaged Russian Empire, communists promptly embarked upon more war, wherever they thought they'd win. Soviet Russia signed the Treaty of Brest-Litovsk with Germany, Austria-Hungary, Bulgaria, and the Ottoman Empire early in 1918, but later that year reneged. (Muslim Turks had already broken the treaty by invading Christian Armenia in May.) Waging war when the rest of Europe found armistice, Russia attacked Estonia, Belarus, Ukraine, and Poland in an offensive aiming to make Europe communist by invasion or revolution. Poland thwarted it in 1921.

In response to the threat of communism when others hesitated, still rattled by war, fascism arose through the 1920s and '30s. Most fascists were peaceful, not harming other races or countries but defending their own. My paternal grandfather, later an officer of the International Red Cross, was a member of the New Guard in Sydney. When the Australian government increased the excise on silk stockings imported from America, he honoured the terms on which he'd agreed to sell a shipment, instead of increasing his prices. It drove him to bankruptcy.

New South Wales fascism meant honouring our commitments: paying our debts rather than reneging from them. Instead of being nationalistic, the New Guard opposed Premier Jack Lang's nationalism, when Australian nationalism meant separation from Britain. Among other responses to the Great Depression, Lang wanted Australia to default on overseas loans until economic conditions improved. Upstaging Lang as he prepared to open the Sydney Harbour Bridge in 1932, Irish-born New Guard leader Francis De Groot rode up on horseback and cut the ribbon with his sword, "in the name of the decent and respectable people of New South Wales."

Lang's dismissal from office and his party's subsequent electoral defeat led to the New Guard waning in popularity. We had no more need for fascism. Lang, forever the nationalist, became an ever more outspoken critic of communism and defender of white Australia. Politics is complex.

Many people through the 1930s admired Germany's dictator rebuilding his broken country. An animal lover and decorated Great War hero, the immigrant from Austria was proving to be one of only two political leaders able to bring his people out of the Great Depression. (The other was the similarly admired Franklin Delano Roosevelt in America.)

If Herr Hitler died then, he might've entered history as among the greatest leaders any country had seen, for what he'd accomplished through his few years in power. Having returned to Germans their self-respect (which their Great War losses gutted and the last of which we beat out of them at Versailles in 1919, and which their many achievements through the time of the Weimar

Republic never really healed), we would've regretted the missed opportunity of all he could have gone onto achieve. The disenfranchising of Jews and their exodus elsewhere might've mattered no more than had previous pogroms in Russia.

Before Britain imagined another war with Germany (let alone the Holocaust), a renegade British voice (a drunkard and womaniser, no less) spoke of the danger Nazi Germany posed. Had we the lexicon then that we've developed of late, we'd have called Winston Churchill a bigot or Naziphobe: the paranoid, lunatic fringe. Being old and from the Conservative Party, he was yesterday's man.

Adolf Hitler didn't die then. Instead, Churchill entered history as among the world's great leaders. Plagued by personal depression he called his "black dog," he would say he never slept better than the night after he became prime minister.

The Russian and Spanish Civil Wars having been smaller wars between communists and nationalists, we speak of World War II as a war against fascism in our first great war of ideology, but fascist dictatorships in Spain and Portugal remained neutral. We left them alone.

Winston Churchill had no problem with fascism as a defence from communism, although he opposed fascism for Britain where communism was not a threat. *"This country gives the impression of discipline, order, goodwill, smiling faces,"* he wrote to his wife, Clementine Churchill, during a visit to Italy, the original Fascist country, in January 1927. *"A happy strict school... The Fascists have been saluting in their impressive manner all over the place."*

Churchill met Fascist dictator Benito Mussolini. He told a press conference in Rome that he had been "charmed" by Mussolini's "gentle and simple bearing" and praised the way "he thought of nothing but the lasting good... of the Italian people." He added that it was "quite absurd to suggest that the Italian Government does not stand upon a popular basis or that it is not upheld by the active and practical assent of the great masses."

In particular, he supported the Fascists' opposition to communism, which he called Leninism. "If I had been an Italian," he said, "I am sure that I should have been whole-heartedly with you from the start to the finish in your triumphant struggle against the bestial appetites and passions of Leninism."

Churchill distinguished Nazism in Germany from fascism in

other countries. On the eighteenth day of October 1930, three years before Hitler became Chancellor of Germany, a Counsellor at the German Embassy in London sent a secret memorandum to his Foreign Ministry, reporting a conversation with Churchill. *"Hitler had admittedly declared that he had no intention of waging a war of aggression; he, Churchill, however, was convinced that Hitler or his followers would seize the first available opportunity to resort to armed force."*

World War II didn't begin in Europe until Germany's expansion reached beyond Czechoslovakia into Poland and threatened to continue. It was another war defending our countries, cultures, and Europe. Germany wanted to save us from communists and Jews. Much as we'd done in the Great War, Britain wanted to save us from Germany.

Britain had long fought wars against any country too powerful. Before the twentieth century, those wars were often against France. Later in the twentieth century, the Cold War would be against the communist Soviet Union. Had the Soviet Union invaded Poland in 1939 imposing communism as it subjugated Eastern Europe from 1945, we'd have declared war on the Soviet Union.

By 1945, we were all too weak from war to continue. Bloodied by two world wars, we had no more mood to fight and die. We'd won our wars and stopped fighting. We'd lost our wars and stopped fighting.

If we declared war on Germany in 1939 to keep Poland free, then the war in Europe was a failure. Poland wouldn't be free until communism collapsed there in 1989. If we presumed Poland's freedom was ours, we were wrong.

We don't question the war because we're taught it was a war against prejudice, but it wasn't at the time. Save only for the Soviet Union seeking to erase races and cultures altogether, racial and religious discrimination were the norm the world over, before and during the war.

My grandfather's enemy wasn't intolerance. It was Germany and Japan.

When British troops entered the Nazi concentration camp at Bergen-Belsen in the last weeks of World War II, British newsreels broadcast images of the dead and dying Jews they found. Narrations calling those images the reason that Britain fought were propaganda inspiring Britons onward, but they would also herald the redefinition of the war into one against prejudice, but only

Western prejudice.

War-end revelations of the Holocaust weren't enough to redefine the war, not for everyone involved. My grandfather respected Germans but, having seen what he'd seen, never ceased being wary of Japanese.

Nor did he cease being a man for God, King or Queen, and Country. God was no generic religion, but Christ Jesus. The King or Queen wasn't monarchy as a system of government, but specifically our British King or Queen. The Country was Australia, indivisible from Britain. Men who'd seen their comrades die didn't surrender their senses of nation.

In 1986, two years after my grandfather died, forty-one years after World War II ended, my girlfriend and I wandered through evening mist in the French hilltop town of Avranches. We stumbled upon a mammoth statue on a stone block that grateful townspeople four decades earlier erected in George Patton's honour. Patton was arguably the most aggressive and combative American general in war, proudly taking more German casualties than any other. Upon Germany's surrender, he stopped fighting.

If the war had been against prejudice, we didn't persuade the people who fought. "*I have been at Frankfurt for a civil government conference,*" Patton wrote to his wife, the last Monday in August, 1945. "*If what we are doing is 'Liberty,' then give me death.' I can't see how Americans can sink so low. It is Semitic, and I am sure of it.*"

From an attempt at genocide came an era of revenge. The war wasn't over.

"*Today we received orders…in which we were told to give the Jews special accommodations,*" he wrote in his diary. "*If for Jews, why not Catholics, Mormons, etc.?*" He went onto mention the enslavement of Germans we soon forgot. "*We are also turning over to the French several hundred thousand prisoners of war to be used as slave labor in France.*"

Patton's view of Germans was kinder than any I've heard since then, particularly from Germans. "*Actually, the Germans are the only decent people left in Europe,*" he wrote the last day of August, 1945. Like others of his time, Patton mightn't have considered Britain to be in Europe. "*It's a choice between them and the Russians. I prefer the Germans.*" The Russia he described was communist.

While others exacted their revenge upon Germans, dismantling Germany, Patton had no wish to punish them more. "*What we are doing is to destroy the only semi-modern state in Europe,*" he wrote the first

Sunday of September 1945, "*so that Russia can swallow the whole.*"

Patton's war wasn't against prejudice or even Nazism. As governor of Bavaria, he allowed Nazis to remain in office, equating them to America's principal political parties. "This Nazi thing," he told a press conference the penultimate Saturday of September 1945, "it's just like a Democratic–Republican election fight."

Nazi Germany couldn't stop Patton. American newspapers could. Their ensuing outrage quickly led to him being removed from office; his saving Europe mattered less than their hatred of Nazis. In December, he died from injuries received in a crash between American military vehicles.

The 1970 American film *Patton* included a scene in which Patton and another soldier walked in cold air among fallen soldier's graves in the sand. They wandered up a small rise from which they looked across the desert, beyond which were German soldiers, graves, and Patton's counterpart, Field Marshal Erwin Rommel. "You know," said Patton, "if I had my way, I'd send that genius son of a bitch an engraved invitation in iambic pentameter: A challenge in two stanzas to meet me out there alone in the desert... Rommel in his tank and me in mine, we'd stop about twenty paces. We'd get out and shake hands. We'd button up and we'd do battle, just the two of us. That battle would decide the outcome of the war."

Such a duel would've saved millions of lives. When I was young, I'd had much the same idea as to how wars could be fought, without so many people dying. World War II in Europe would have been a bout between Churchill and Hitler, without armies or countries. The two men could've fought with guns, swords, or their bare hands in a private room, field, or stadium before crowds of their countrymen; whatever they wanted. I imagined neither man being so quick to risk his life as he was to condemn his compatriots to die.

"Too bad jousting's gone out of style," the other soldier in the film replied to Patton. "It's like your poetry, General. It isn't part of the twentieth century."

I hope Patton really said those words, or something like so romantic an ideal. Rommel might've accepted the invitation. Among the injured in a German hospital Rommel inspected was a British Army soldier Jim McConnell. Rommel spoke with him as gentlemen spoke, respecting him. Decades later, that soldier was the schoolmaster I knew as Jock.

Rommel defied orders to kill captured Jewish soldiers, and was implicated in a plot to kill Hitler in 1944. For his prestige, Hitler allowed him to commit suicide; some prestige.

Looking back six decades later, Rommel wasn't our impression of the people we'd been fighting. Patton wasn't our impression of the people we'd been.

Reminding me that the war wasn't against prejudice, Patton and his fellow soldier in the film walked back towards their soldiers' graves. "I want a twenty-four hour guard put around this area," said Patton. "Those damned Arabs will dig them out, just to get their clothes."

Soon enough, the favours we granted Jews we granted other races and their religions. With ideologies ignited by the Great War debacle burning more fiercely than ever, the cruellest conflicts in the world became those between white people.

Communism fell in Eastern Europe in 1989. The Soviet Union collapsed in 1991. Whatever Marxism then came to mean, it remained a rejection of Western cultures, societies, and civilisation. Understanding the West of the early twenty-first century requires recognising the extraordinary indifference and animosity white people (and not simply the Marxists) feel towards their race and culture.

Normally hiding from public shaming and punishment, or simply too weak, tired, or uncertain of themselves to resist, are Western nationalists: caring for their countries, cultures, and races. In control are the globalists, the multiculturalists: neglectful and often belligerent towards Western countries, cultures, and races. It's the tussle between support and separation, self-belief and self-loathing, self-determination and self-destruction. It's the struggle between trying to move on from two world wars and remaining in the mire.

There's no greater burden upon people than espousing loyalty to those who scold us for our loyalty, but our people are no less our people for being disloyal. Ideologies are unnatural, which is why nationalism, nativism, racism, and other tribalism aren't ideologies. Western socialism, capitalism, conservatism, and liberalism that were nationalist and racist became multiculturalist. What had been competing ideas for advancing civilisation became ideological, uninterested in our countries and cultures.

No other race is so inimical to its own, to anyone who'd save it. Ours is a uniquely Western conflict: an internecine clash in which other races side with whomever suits them. They're comfortable with their countries, cultures, and races: their racism and nationalism. Some contemptuous of Western nationalism became sympathetic in the face of Muslim terror.

Other races now harm us with our concurrence. It's one thing to have an idea, such as all cultures being equal, or the dream of a single world civilisation. It's quite another to hold steadfast to that dream or idea when people are dying. That's ideology.

Multiculturalism fails because it's predicated upon individualism, however much the noble and ignoble wish otherwise. Individualism fails because individuals are small, whether in fine homes with deep principles or in caravans with broken wheels. No matter how much smarter, stronger, or richer an individual may be over another, the cumulative capacities of races and nations exceed those of individuals. A stupid, weak, and poor population prevails over wise, robust, and wealthy individuals by the force of numbers, the weight of so many: the rule of nations. A solitary person, however brilliant and able, is no match for a mob.

The world is no place for individuals. When we renounced Western Civilisation, we left spaces to be filled.

There will never be a global civilisation as the West understands civilisation to be. The rest of the world doesn't want it. If there ever is a world civilisation, then it'll be because a race or league of races imposes it. Rights, religion, and everything else will be for that race or league, not us, to determine.

The inevitable outcome of multiculturalism is our submission to self-confident, collective peoples. The most self-certain, collective religion on earth is Islam.

Whatever the majority of Muslims thinks hardly matters. Be they races, collective religions, nations, or anything else, tribes aren't driven by the majority. The masses busy with their daily lives (working, feeding their families, or playing) follow or acquiesce. Tribes are driven by the few with power and zeal. We are.

2. THE UNFINISHED WAR

Sometime through the late 1970s or early '80s, the Hitler's World Tour tee shirt appeared at first sight like keepsakes sold for musical concerts, except that the face and figure emblazoned on the front were Adolf Hitler's. The rear of the shirt, as such shirts did, listed several countries, but they weren't venues for concerts. They were countries Nazi Germany, the Third Reich, fought. The last tour spots, Britain and Russia, were marked *"Cancelled."*

The tee shirts mocked the dead dictator, exemplifying our obsession with him so many years on, unwilling to let the war end. The uproar when newspapers learned of them illustrated the frenzy of sensitivity around our fixation. My neighbour Paul Hanke knew a Jew condemning them in the media, although he told Paul he did so because other Jews expected it of him. His son wore the shirt. I wore one, too.

While communists who'd won the old Russian Empire in 1917 and Eastern Europe in 1945 lost them in 1989 and '91, World War II became the fractured West's definitive war: the war upon which we dwell (if we dwell upon any), as if there's never been another. For all our talk of hating war, we have no problem with tens of millions of Europeans dying, now that we're not among them. World War II became the West's unfinished war.

In November 1986, more than four decades after Hitler's death, my girlfriend and I were in the Pergamon Museum, communist East Berlin. World War II bombs had damaged the Pergamon Temple stone structures, since which time they'd been carefully restored. The ancient Greek mosaic floor didn't make the same impression on us that it made on an American woman. "My God!" her accent screamed aghast, like a people at war. "It's a swastika! It's a goddamned swastika!"

I looked again at the intricate pattern in the tiles. In the intersection of long lines thousands of years old, I slowly discerned a semblance of a swastika, the Nazi symbol. Museum guards walked towards her. I moved away.

The four square arms of the swastika had become the most reviled symbol on earth. Half a decade or so later, a vandal used plumber's tar to swipe a swastika across the front door to my home unit. A history schoolteacher, later my wife (although not merely for being a history teacher), realised the swastika arms pointed in the wrong direction. A real Nazi, if any were left, wouldn't have scrawled it.

Perhaps the vandal had responded to the note on the building noticeboard about the resident of my unit number parking a car on common property. Perhaps it was for me being an increasingly rare white face in Meadowbank; the swastika symbolised everything the world saw wrong with white people. Most likely, it was simply something to scrawl.

Our obsession with Hitler was never more obvious, and never more ridiculous, than when global attention turned to Clive Davies' house in Port Tennant, South Wales in 2011. Someone dubbed it the "Hitler house," but not because Hitler visited. Comedian Jimmy Carr was among many to see the Führer's features in the masonry: a dark front door below a thin canopy, windows spaced equally to the sides like eyes, and a sloping roof like a hairline. Gentiles as much as Jews recognised Hitler's short, square black moustache and black parted hair. I couldn't. Then again, my home also had a dark front door.

"Some people say they can see images of Jesus Christ on items such as toast, and I suppose it is just a variation on a theme," said Davies. "I don't really think it looks like Hitler."

The Hitler house would come to seem self-evident, compared to the ruckus when American retailer JC Penney advertised a Bells and Whistles stainless steel kettle along the 405 interstate highway near Culver City, California, in May 2013. Motorists took photographs copied around the world, because they thought the kettle in silhouette looked like Hitler.

The rest of Western history has gone, leaving little more than Hitler standing. Commenting upon the 2012 Emmy Awards ceremony, Jewish journalist Nikki Finke acerbically described the History Channel on American television as having been the Hitler Channel. An award for *Hatfields & McCoys* made it, that year only, the Hatfield Channel.

"I grew up wanting to kill Nazis," said American actor Tom Cruise in 2008. His ancestry was Welsh, not Jewish, and he was born in 1962: seventeen years after the war ended. Cruise was talking about his role in the film *Valkyrie*, which told the true story of a German officer plotting to kill Hitler. Cruise had been surprised to learn there'd been such plots.

Refusing to consider any real, present-day threat and being told forever how wicked we used to be, our war against Nazis is a rare part of Western history in which we're free to feel pride. We're not free to fight other races or cultures and too frightened to do so, but Nazis offer us mythical foes. In our endless war-footing, we're ready to fight them knowing we'll never meet them.

My twelve-year-old eldest son, born more than half a century after the war ended, enthused for killing Nazis without contemplating war with anyone else. That might've had something to do with his devotion to the *Star Wars* films, in which heroes fought faceless, white storm troopers. (Nazi storm troopers wore black, which must have seemed racist by the time *Star Wars* appeared.)

In 1994, my colleague Dick McDonald gave me a copy of the *Wolfenstein 3-D* computer game. A gently mannered fellow with a loving devoted family, Dick warned me the game was addictive, as his brother giving him the game warned him, but a course in managerial psychology through my studies for a Master of Business Administration degree convinced me there was no such thing as addiction, not mental addiction anyway. Some people want some things over and over.

Alone for the weekend, I began playing the game Saturday. Not simply sitting at my computer in the spare bedroom of my two-bedroom apartment, I was racing through the mythical Castle Wolfenstein on a hero's brave mission, shooting grotesque, soulless Nazis before they shot me. More kept appearing. I collected treasures, food supplies, and medical kits, soon learning to hug walls searching for them, between killing Nazis. All afternoon I sat there, wanting to play a little bit more before setting off to a friend's party that evening.

Dusk came and I continued playing, knowing I could be a little bit late for the party. Onward I played, getting later, the night becoming darker, until finally I stopped. I never did get to Gillian's party.

Knowing I had a problem, I soon stopped playing the game altogether. Among the people who played it repeatedly was Michael

McDermott (born Michael Martinez). He murdered seven fellow workers at the Edgewater Technology site in Wakefield, Massachusetts the day after Christmas Day, 2000. McDermott told his trial he believed he was living inside something like Castle Wolfenstein. "The last Nazi was there," he testified, of the state of his mind. "I shot and killed him, and Hitler was there. I shot and killed him. My mission was complete. I knew at this point I had a soul."

No reports suggested any of his victims were Nazis, Germans, or racists. They might just have been white.

Vengeful Jews and we hunt down former Nazis until the end of their lives. An accountant at the Auschwitz concentration camp, Oskar Gröning never killed anyone. He simply sorted banknotes from Jewish arrivals. The British punished him with forced labour after World War II, when he was indicted for war crimes. As the threat from Soviet communism grew, we helped West Germany rebuild. Gröning wasn't prosecuted at the time. Most forced labour of Germans ended early in the 1950s.

By 2015, seventy years after the war ended, we only feared Nazism. A German court sentenced Gröning, ninety-four years of age, to four years in gaol for being complicit in the murder of Jews.

Other state-sanctioned killers enjoy partial or complete amnesties. East Europeans didn't pursue most of the communists after communism collapsed there. In Colombia, the Justice and Peace process capped gaol sentences to just eight years, even for Jorge Ivan Laverde, a commander in the United Self Defence Forces of Colombia militia, dismantled in 2003. In 2010, he admitted to killing a hundred people and ordering the killings of four thousand others.

We're uninterested in communist atrocities. Estimates vary widely, but in pursuit of power and implementing communist ideology, Soviet dictator Joseph Stalin killed somewhere between five and seventy million Russians, Ukrainians, and others from 1924 until his death in '53. The most commonly cited total is around about twenty million dead.

Estimates of the numbers of Chinese and others killed by communist dictator Mao Zedong from 1949 until his death in '76 also vary widely. The most commonly cited total is around forty million dead.

From 1975 until '79, dictator Pol Pot (born Saloth Sar, who'd studied radio electronics in France in his youth) sought to create a perfect communist, agrarian state in Cambodia, banning religion. Communists murdered anyone tainted with the old order of capitalism, including those close to Western interests. Outside the West and Soviet Union, communism (like everything else) remained nationalistic and racist, with the regime also targeting Chinese (who'd been disproportionately shopkeepers), Vietnamese, and Laotians, along with intellectuals and disabled people. Again estimates vary widely, but over the four years of the Khmer Rouge regime, executions and government policies probably killed a quarter of the Cambodian population, if not more.

No idealists and ideologues were more brutal than communists, but killings by communists haven't eaten away at equality or other ideology the way our revulsion at the Holocaust destroyed Western nationalism and racism. Motive matters. We treat mass murder for ideological reasons, which most massacres through the twentieth century were, as being less wrongful than killing people for their race. I'm not sure the victims differentiate.

There's no ideological guilt, only ideological innocence accorded the opponents of nationalism. While Soviet communism lost the Cold War economically to capitalism, it won the political conflict against a West still shaken by war and scarred by holocaust. Our postmodern West is a hybrid communist-capitalism predicated upon ideologies, without nation, race, or religion in play. We're trapped in our construction of 1945, frozen at the open gates of Birkenau.

We've accepted, even admired, communists such as the last leader of the Soviet Union, Mikhail Gorbachev, while ostracising democratically elected nationalists like Austria's President Kurt Waldheim and Governor Jörg Haider. *"We see how the Left has won the Cold War,"* wrote English journalist Boris Johnson of Haider in 2000, so striking has been our contrasting attitudes. *"The evils of communism are quietly sponged from the record, and we whip ourselves into a frenzy about an allegedly fascist clown…and all because he is an Austrian whose surname begins with H and ends with R."*

For all our self-righteousness, a monster in our body politic enjoys hating. A person who marshals that monster can mobilise the masses against anyone, in the name of smashing such hatred. What we call a war against hatred isn't a war against hatred, because we hate fascists.

In 1939, countries were communist (like the Soviet Union including Russia, Ukraine, and Belarus), fascist (like Germany including Austria, Hungary, Italy, Spain, and Portugal), or nationalist democracies. Most were nationalist democracies. By equating fascism with nationalism, we've lost the option of liberal nationalism.

If fascism is any nationalist authoritarianism, then a myriad of fascist regimes have arisen around the world. If fascism encompasses racist democracies, there are even more. They don't concern us. We only imagine white people being fascists. We only equate white racism and nationalism with fascism.

The post-racial, post-religious, post-national future we demand is for white people only. Other races agree.

Soviet communism was totalitarianism without racism or nationalism (except when defence from Nazi Germany required them through World War II), so we don't call it fascism. Multiculturalism is the same. My friend Robert spoke proudly of crushing the fascists in the New South Wales Liberal Party in the 1980s. They were people he thought weren't liberal, although they might just have been not liberal enough or liberal about the wrong things.

We're so quick to describe white racists as fascists, we don't imagine we're driving them to sympathise with fascism. We're certain they already do. If they're not wholeheartedly embracing other races and cultures, surrendering their own, they must be fascists. We know how to deal with fascists.

We deem all manner of authorities to be fascists, and the worst of them to be Nazis. My wife described the cruellest of school boarding staff mistresses as Nazis, as I'm sure they never called themselves.

In a 1995 episode of the American television series *Seinfeld*, Jewish comedian Jerry Seinfeld described the owner of a soup stand as being a Soup Nazi for the regime he imposed upon customers. The soup was so good, the customers kept returning, but still hated the Soup Nazi.

(The series' final episode revealed his name to be Yev Kassem, but the actor playing him, born Larry Tomashoff, was three-quarters Russian and one-quarter Romanian. Ali Yeganeh, the Iranian Jew upon whom the character was based, took great offence at the moniker.)

From the perspectives of other races and our endless individualism, fascism has come to mean any structures of a Western society. American actor Paul Giamatti, who played the role of a police inspector, described the early 1900s Vienna portrayed in the 2006 American film *The Illusionist* as "fascistic."

The characters Tim and Debbie in the 1980s satirical television series *Australia You're Standing in it* complained about traffic lights. "Like," said Debbie, "in the olden days, right, um all you had to do was just get on your animal and just carve your own road between where your head was at and where you wanted it to be."

"Right," agreed Tim, "and these days, it's traffic lights, right: fascist traffic lights. It's either stop, or go, walk or don't walk, and there's no, like, range of emotional responses."

In 2015, the Victorian government banned children who'd not been vaccinated from kindergarten and childcare, to protect other children. Melbourne cartoonist Michael Leunig, of German ancestry, called it a "fascist epiphany." He did so with a cartoon mimicking Michelangelo's fresco *The Creation of Adam*, but with one hand holding a needle. Public health had become fascism.

Immigrants asserting their cultures, refusing to accede to their hosts, become our allies against fascism. In her 2012 article "Your in America' sets grammar fascists against fascists,' Arwa Mahdawi described Americans wanting people in America to speak English as fascists. She described people wanting correct English grammar as grammar fascists.

With such a meaning of fascism, we were all fascists in 1939. Nobody went to war for the freedom to make grammatical errors.

3. MULTICULTURALISM AT WAR

The most common prayer the West pleas is for peace. Come Christmas and Easter with more reason than ever to dwell upon God, life, and death, our messages are peace; the dove is the symbol we set forth to the world. We are the kindest, gentlest people on earth.

Just not with each other. The most striking feature of the world isn't that there should be racial or religious tension, even conflict, but that, where it involves white people, we've become so quick to side with other races and religions. We buy into battles to battle our own.

Despite Rhodesia's origins as a fellow British colony, Australia's Prime Minister Malcolm Fraser was among the supposedly Eminent People working to end white minority rule there in the late 1970s. My Polish acquaintance Ryk had a friend in the Australian Army, a major then, thought Ryk, who gave Fraser a detailed briefing of the atrocities attributable to black leader Robert Mugabe, including a one-page executive summary. Fraser calmly tore up the summary. He threw the thick briefing away.

Tribal conflicts during the first decade of black rule in Zimbabwe caused at least twenty thousand deaths. Increasing hostility and violence against white people through the decades included several brutal murders of farmers. "Don't they know where their ancestors came from?" Mugabe asked in 2014. "The British who are here should all go back to England."

When we lost our racial loyalties, we didn't stop harming white people. We stopped saving them.

With a cathedral under construction and community so rare in the West, Belgrade was more European than other Western cities remained by 1991. Fine old stone buildings stood over elegant shopping malls and precincts, along which I walked freely. A few days later, the fighting between Serbs and Croats elsewhere in formerly communist Yugoslavia was more reason for the West to hate nationalism, but there was no fighting when formerly communist Czechoslovakia split into two countries in 1993.

'93 was the year that American Japanese political economist Francis Fukuyama (married to a white American, Laura Holmgren) published *The End of History and the Last Man*. Fukuyama argued that political and economic conflict was over, Western liberalism had prevailed over communism, and there would become, in effect, a single world civilisation. It was Hegelian dualism reminiscent of Karl Marx and his conviction that history ended with communism. Having brought on board someone from another race can only have added to our sense of certainty.

American political scientist Samuel Huntington rejected Fukuyama's thesis, in a lecture at the American Enterprise Institute and then an article titled 'The Clash of Civilisations?' He warned of the world returning to the cultural clashes it experienced before the ideological conflicts of the twentieth century.

The West's willingness to give up our races and cultures for world unity haven't made other races willing to give up theirs. Still believing in the roles of religion and race, they've retained their racism, nationalism, and other loyalties. Islam separates the world into *Dar al-Harb* (the countries of chaos) and *Dar al-Islam*.

"I wouldn't want to create the impression that I wouldn't like the government of the United States to be Islamic sometime in the future," Ibrahim Hooper told a reporter for the *Minneapolis Star-Tribune* newspaper on the fourth of April 1993. He later became national spokesman for the Council on America–Islamic Relations.

"The Koran…should be the highest authority in America and Islam the only accepted religion on earth," were a reporter's paraphrasing of words that Omar Ahmad, a founder of the Council on America–Islamic Relations, told a conference hall filled with California Muslims in July 1998.

Conflicts around capitalism and communism between European peoples had passed. Our Age of Ideology had not.

Multiculturalism remains, if only for regions of the West spared the experience of Soviet communism. Also in 1993, Ed Vulliamy, Britain's Foreign Correspondent of the Year, wrote in the *Guardian* newspaper of being with Muslim Bosnians fighting Christian Serbs. "*My father had the honour of fighting fascism; I instead have the strange privilege of meeting the people who are fighting a pale but unmistakable imitation of the Third Reich.*"

Forty-eight years after Nazi Germany's defeat, we wanted the war we thought our fathers and grandfathers fought. The title of Vulliamy's article described 'A destiny worse than war.'

Journalist Chris Hedges covered the conflicts in the crumbling Yugoslavia for the *New York Times* newspaper. "*Many of us, restless and unfulfilled, see no supreme worth in our lives,*" he wrote in his 2002 book *War Is a Force That Gives Us Meaning*, "*...war, at least gives a sense that we can rise above our smallness and divisiveness.*"

We're still fighting wars, but not as we did and other races do. We're the siblings at arms, but armed against each other still believing, or again believing, in nation, race, or collective Christianity. We're fighting the white nationalists we wish we'd fought before 1939.

The Great War began in 1914 with Russia, France, and Britain defending Serbia against Austria-Hungary and Germany. Eighty-five years later, we had no currency with Serbia defending herself from Muslim insurgency. Calling them Kosovars made them locals instead of immigrants, but the criminals, terrorists, and revolutionaries of the Kosovo Liberation Army were racially Albanians. We wanted them free to stay within Serbian borders fighting to secede from Serbia, rather than fleeing the fighting to return to Albania. Both sides committed wrongs in that cruel civil war, but our eyes were upon Serbs. They weren't upon Albanians.

Britain's Prime Minister Tony Blair championed a new type of war, but it was an old war, World War II, revisited in our anti-national, anti-racial, anti-religious image. It might have spun from Blair's British history of fair play, but was not fair play. It might have spun from his postmodern, multicultural Christianity, without racial or religious loyalty, without Christianity.

Being the humanitarians we are, we called it humanitarian war. We're still the world's policemen and, being British, presume we are the nice policemen, but we are not so nice with white nationalists as we are with everyone else.

America's Albright Doctrine also employed military force for supposedly moral objectives. Born in Prague in 1937, Madeleine Albright was raised a Roman Catholic before fleeing Nazis and then communists. She'd become American ambassador to the United Nations in 1993 and secretary of state in 1997, about which time she learned she was three-quarters Jewish.

Albright was among the foreign ministers at a conference in

London in 1998 debating the Serbian action in Kosovo, when her aide Jamie Rubin suggested she might accept the soft language threatening the Serbs suggested by the French and Italian ministers. "Where do you think we are," she retorted, "Munich?" In the 1938 Munich Agreement, Britain, France, and Italy averted war by allowing Hitler's Germany to annex portions of Czechoslovakia in which ethnic Germans lived.

With what we devotedly call our ideals, German Greens replaced their slogan of "No more wars," with "No more Auschwitz." Believing in a world without boundaries, it's hard to think of any other reason to fight.

America, Britain, and their allies bombed Serbia to support Kosovars in 1999: civil war in Christendom, a wilful war waged against a European people, dropping bombs upon intolerance no longer of Jews but of Muslims. When bombs proved inadequate to force Serbian troop withdrawal from her province, we threatened invasion.

Quicker to fight Serbia than we'd fought Nazi Germany, we fought as fervently as our forebears fought, but not for God and Country, at least not ours. We fight for other people, their god, and country: multiculturalism at war. We're not saving Europe, at least for Europeans, but saving others from Europe. Aiding Kosovars by killing hundreds of Serbs, we felt prouder than we'd felt for generations.

Serbian troops withdrew. The Kosovars then expelled Serbs and other racial and religious minorities from Kosovo, but we didn't intervene to save Serbs. Defending Christian Europeans would've been racist. We're too preoccupied with white peoples' intolerance to notice what other races do.

World war and holocaust we consider Western crimes. Muslim crime and terrorism pale by comparison.

We're unconcerned about the races and religions we embolden, wishing we'd been unconcerned when we didn't fight Nazi Germany during the 1930s for fear of Soviet communism. We're far more fearful of Europe's prejudice, and far more vengeful towards it. We've lost the concept of any race or culture but our own being a danger.

I didn't read or hear of it at the time, but Macedonia suffered a similar conflict in 2001, as I learnt eight years later. My second daughter's friend Marina and her parents were Macedonian. While the children continued playing after a party in their apartment, her father Nash, Claire's father, and I drank from bottles of Heineken beer in their kitchen area. Nash spoke glowingly of life in the former Yugoslavia, where people were kind to strangers and there was a strong moral and ethical code to the country. Communism never sounded so good, but he spoke of nationalism.

I'd drunk thick black coffee with Macedonians in Nash's hometown Skopje in 1993, when Serbia had imposed sanctions on Macedonia for seceding from Yugoslavia and Greece had imposed sanctions on Macedonia because she objected to the name. Albanians in Macedonia moved with arrogance aloof from Macedonians, except to rob them.

By 2001, Nash told me, Albanians had also become terrorists. Several hundred people died in fighting between Macedonians and Albanians, but every time the Macedonians surrounded a group of terrorists in a village, the Americans telephoned the Macedonian leadership and threatened to bomb Macedonia if they attacked the Albanians. Having seen the killing in Serbia, the Macedonians backed down.

Enforcing racial and religious diversity in Europe, we expected Serbs and Macedonians to tolerate crime and terror by other races and religions, as we do; sympathising with crime and terrorism shouldn't be a crime. We refuse to respond with prejudice. So should they. We demanded Serbs and Macedonians treat Albanians as individuals with individual rights, punishing Serbs collectively when they didn't. We won't wage war with other races or religions, but we'll bash our own to the death.

I imagined our instinctive support of racial minorities throughout the West had moved the Americans, but Nash linked it to Albanians forming a Mafia at least as bad as the Sicilian crime families. Prostitution, crime, and corruption were among the moral breakdown that came with the coming of individualism to Yugoslavia.

The second last Tuesday of July 2007, I took my three eldest children and eldest son's Persian friend David to see the film *Harry Potter and the Order of the Phoenix*. Tuesdays were the days for cheap cinema tickets in Sydney and particularly cheap tickets there, although we still managed to spend fifty-five dollars. The manager then refused my thirsty eleven-year-old son a cup of tap water, wanting us to spend two more dollars to buy bottled water.

Yet, there'd been no such grumbling accorded me fourteen years earlier, in the remnants of Yugoslavia. Poor, nationalist Serbia was a Western pariah, but long-distance trains needed to pass through the country. Travelling from Skopje to Sofia, I spent two hours of a hot day between services in Niš. Western sanctions prevented me exchanging my money for otherwise-worthless Yugoslav currency, but no international economic or political conflict deterred a Serbian cafeteria waitress from giving a weary traveller a glass of cold, clean tap water.

More than seventeen hundred years earlier, Niš was the birthplace of Constantine, the first Roman emperor to convert to Christianity. On the first Friday of May 1999, as part of our attacks on Serbs to aid Kosovars, Dutch aircraft dropped cluster bombs on Niš, killing civilians. If bombing Serbia was a "battle between good and evil, between civilisation and barbarity," as Blair said in a speech in Chicago, then we were the barbarians. If totalitarianism is the use of force to impose our will upon others, then we'd become the oppressors. I never learnt what happened to that kind cafeteria waitress.

Rarely has a Western government since World War II defended her people and countries as the Serbian and Macedonian governments tried to do. Increasingly, we submit our citizens to the world, certain of the justice we do. What had been our call for God and Country became our call for the multicultural globe, to which we expect each other to subscribe. We live for our new global ideal we value above each other's lives, consequently our own. We no longer defend ourselves or each other. We can't so much as stand up for ourselves.

Fixated with fighting white prejudice, it's hard to see what we support, except everyone else. (Boy, am I in trouble.)

We presume to hate war, but we're fighting World War II as if it weren't yet won: fighting each other as if the other were a dictator who died and regime that ended in 1945. We fight each other over race and religion, while refusing to fight other races and religions. Instead of fighting other people's intolerance of us, we're fighting white people's intolerance of others. Our forebears fought foreigners to defend and restore European borders. We fight each other to ensure those borders aren't restored again.

Redefining old wars won't be an issue for future generations looking back at ours. We don't die for anything; we employ soldiers to die. War with Serbia in the 1990s was a faraway war not affecting us in our homes. It didn't change anything about our lives. All we do is wage abuse upon each other, thinking we're better than our forebears who fought. We seize upon every little question mark over each other's ideology: talk of defending our countries and ways of life at odds with our vision of a single world people.

Wars haven't stopped because we stopped defending ourselves, but for the first time in Western history (as Australian Army chaplain Father Rob pointed out in a sermon at our parish Anglican church for Anzac Day, 2012), we're sending our soldiers to war without conviction in God. Through past wars our peoples had Christian conviction, even if individuals among us did not.

Michael Weinstein, an American Jew, formed the Military Religious Freedom Foundation in 2005. The freedom he espoused was his own. He accused Christians in the American military, including chaplains, sharing their faith of treason and "spiritual rape" as serious as sexual assault. In 2013, the military threatened court martial for soldiers proselyting any religion.

The West doesn't fear Muslims. We fear Christians.

If other races send their soldiers to war without religious conviction, they at least send them with conviction in their countries, cultures, and people. They're not dying for anyone else. The only reason for people to risk their lives protecting each other is nationalism or other tribalism. When people are being killed, war against a people's nationalism is war against that people.

4. SEPTEMBER ELEVEN, 2001

The West's acceptance of refugees and other immigrants and our provision of trillions of dollars in foreign aid and domestic welfare payments bring us little, if any, favour from other races. Our support for Afghans fighting the Soviet Union through the 1980s and for Albanians through the 1990s brought us no favour from Muslims. We don't expect them to. We don't think in such terms. We bombed Serbia and threatened Macedonia because we hated white intolerance so much.

I didn't read or hear Samuel Huntington's predictions of a clash of civilisations when he wrote them or, if I did, I forgot them. We lived the Francis Fukuyama confidence without realising it, although in 1998, Fukuyama was a signatory to a letter from the Project for the New American Century recommending that President Bill Clinton support insurgents trying to overthrow Iraqi dictator Saddam Hussein. His views would continue to evolve, if not change altogether.

On Tuesday, the eleventh of September 2001, I joined several of my former colleagues from Holyman Limited through the evening, Sydney time, in the Forbes Hotel. Patrons wearing business shirts, skirts, and suits stood at the brass-fitted serving area filling the middle of the main bar. Others sat in the booths around the walls or, if they were lucky, the few iron chairs along the side of the footpath. Dark timber fittings and carpets made the bars seem more crowded, upstairs and down. I returned home too tired to check the television news.

In the morning, I stood in my pyjamas at my wife's and my bedroom window, contemplating the work that builders were close to completing in our back garden. There seemed no end of problems with them setting the higher steps narrower than I'd wanted or erecting the lower steps away from the cliff. My wife had risen earlier than I had and appeared at the door. "Have you seen the news?" she asked me.

The small television set in our bedroom was off. "No."

"It's on every channel." Our children were unable to watch their usual morning programmes. "Something's happened in America."

I switched on the television set. My life had been without war, at least in Australia and America, but I stared disbelieving at the burning wreck of two of the world's tallest buildings: the twin towers of the World Trade Centre, New York. They'd been offices, no different to those in which my friends and I worked.

Six years earlier, almost to the day, I'd first visited America. Friday afternoon in New York, I'd grabbed a short time between meetings to visit the observation floor high in one of the twin towers, from which other buildings and Newark were adornments to view. In spite of its great height, the sprawling expanse in which I stood seemed perfectly solid and secure. Six years on, the white towers smouldered in rubble.

Nineteen Muslim Arabs, of whom many had lived and studied in America, had simultaneously hijacked four domestic aircraft bound from America's east coast to her west. They'd given no warning, made no demands. Laden with fuel for long flights, the Arabs crashed two aeroplanes into the twin towers in New York and a third into the Pentagon military headquarters in Washington. The fourth was headed to Washington to kill more people when the passengers, alerted by mobile telephone to the other suicide attacks, risked their lives already lost to overcome the hijackers. In the ensuing fracas, the aircraft crashed into a Pennsylvania field.

The hijackers hadn't just wanted to destroy buildings. They acted on a working Tuesday morning to maximise the numbers of deaths. Holyman Limited's subsidiary chartered commuter ferries operating between Atlantic Highlands, New Jersey and Lower Manhattan. No employees died that day, but many of the cars that passengers had parked by the Atlantic Highlands terminal that morning, as they'd parked them every weekday morning to ferry to work, remained until their family or friends retrieved them.

Three thousand people, most of them like me, died that morning. Among the dead were hundreds of New York firefighters, who'd entered the burning towers to help survivors escape before the towers collapsed. They perished heroes, trying to save people's lives, but in his acrimony towards Americans, Australian commentator Philip Adams abused the dead firefighters for arrogance.

Television stations repeated the mesmerising images trying to make them real: aircraft against a blue sky in autumn flying into the towers, exploding, and those towers crashing down. A few days later, at a gathering for parents of my eldest son's kindergarten class, the attacks dominated conversation. One mother told us her child watching the images assured her, "Don't be scared, Mummy. It isn't real."

Americans rushed out to buy books about Islam trying to understand why Muslims hated them. Muslims didn't buy books about America.

Expert opinion quickly laid blame for the attacks on al-Qaeda, a Muslim terrorist organisation owing its origins to ferocious Muslim assaults upon Soviet troops propping up the communist government in Afghanistan through the 1980s, when the ideological threat from communism made Muslims our allies. With our Western presumption people are all one and the same and really quite reasonable, a Melbourne radio announcer reportedly suggested America respond to the 2001 attacks by sitting down with al-Qaeda to understand Muslim grievances, presumably over scones, cream, and jam.

Most races on earth cast collective guilt upon other races and religions doing them harm. Not us, not since the Holocaust. We cast guilt upon us, collectively blaming ourselves.

Australian journalist Peter FitzSimons apologised on behalf of the world to al-Qaeda and other Muslims for causing the *"incredible suffering"* that *"drove the planes into the World Trade Centre towers."* (Our rejection of race and nation keeps thinking we are the world, but I'm sure he meant only the West.) Since the 1990s, Western and other countries had imposed sanctions on Iraq for expelling United Nations inspectors checking whether it was developing weapons of mass destruction. No evidence linked those sanctions with the 2001 attacks.

The attacks made America more popular than she'd been for years; we love victims. Instead of basking in our sympathy, she snapped awake from her slumber. She aided rebels fighting the Muslim Taliban government in Kabul that abetted al-Qaeda. She prepared to attack al-Qaeda training camps in Afghanistan before more terrorists came. Many a white person, including my multilingual secretary Liz from Holyman Limited, objected, insisting an Afghan or anyone else's life was worth as much as an

American's life, as only we without loyalties would.

Two years earlier, Balkan lives hadn't all been the same worth. People who'd wanted us to kill Serbs to protect Albanians didn't want us killing Afghans to protect Americans. Defending our own would be nationalism.

With every military response, America's popularity waned. The more she dared to fight back, no longer the victim but the warrior, the more unpopular she became.

A month after the atrocities, Australia suffered a federal election. Opposing the American and allied military response to al-Qaeda in Afghanistan was a man handing out Greens political brochures at the Killara High School polling booth. He said the Americans should negotiate with al-Qaeda.

"How can they negotiate when al-Qaeda never actually made any demands?" I asked him.

"We don't even know if it was al-Qaeda."

I might've pointed to the illogic of negotiations with people who denied responsibility anyway as al-Qaeda often did, before eventually boasting of it. I might've walked away rather than waste my time I should spend talking with voters.

Conspiracy theorists blame Western (particularly American) governments for anything bad, rather than blame other races. As they would, they'd already decided the Americans concocted the attacks. Like all good conspiracies, the less evidence it existed, then the bigger the conspiracy must be. This one was gargantuan.

I heard no Western leader associate the atrocities with race or religion, bar one indiscretion. "We should be confident of the superiority of our civilisation," said Italy's Prime Minister Silvio Berlusconi in Berlin, the Wednesday a week afterwards, "which consists of a value system that has given people widespread prosperity and guarantees respect for human rights and religion. This respect certainly does not exist in Islamic countries."

Arab countries demanded an apology. Western leaders distanced themselves from the comment. *Time* magazine called it a gaffe. Berlusconi said he'd been misunderstood.

The details of Berlusconi's words didn't filter through well. In simplistic terms, the news was of him calling the conflict with Islam a clash between civilisations. Samuel Huntington's analysis eight years earlier came to light.

Eight years later, at the Blue Gum Hotel interviewing a

businessman seeking political office, I recalled Berlusconi's words. "Do you think it's a clash of civilisations?" I asked Paul.

Paul was a graduate of Harvard Business School, a Christian of faith, and a father. He replied, "We can't let it be."

So we don't. No mere matter of civilisation is going to interrupt business.

Another businessman candidate, also named Paul, said much the same thing. He spoke proudly of the federal government recently turfed from office surreptitiously increasing immigration.

The day the towers fell, I thought the world had changed. I was wrong. People spoke of tall buildings never again being built, but they were.

As we sat together for lunch around about 2002, Ivo told me of Muslims dancing in the streets of Sydney to celebrate the attacks that day in 2001. Our media reported only Muslim community leaders publicly condemning those attacks. We insist Muslims condemning crime and terror represent all Muslims, while renegade imams who yell their anger at us so loudly and often they can't help but occasionally be reported are recalcitrant individuals.

We have reason to whether our British war against Nazi Germany was worthwhile, given the immense cost it wreaked upon us and upon Europe, but we don't question the last war on our soils. We question the next. In 2002, American television stations broadcasting the 1985 film *Back to the Future* edited out references to criminals being Libyan for fear of offending Arabs.

Serbs thought we'd understand what they'd been dealing with in Kosovo, but we refused to understand. "Disgusting Serbs," screamed Madeleine Albright at protesters at her book signing in the Luxor bookshop in Prague in 2012. "Get out!" Things hardly changed at all.

The anti-religious West doesn't understand religion. We call militant Islam an ideology because we understand ideologies, like communism, multiculturalism, and humanism, but religions aren't ideologies. Muslims believe they act with the authority of Allah, revealed in the Koran and other texts. Ideologies have only human authority, weak as that is. Western secularity can't comprehend religious conviction.

Our blindness to race and religious difference leaves us unprepared for a world that sees. We who've abandoned collective identities are ill prepared to fight people who've retained theirs.

Our disloyalties leave us unable to deal with people of loyalty.

Of all the conflicts the West's rejection of race, cultural difference, and nation since the Holocaust refuse to acknowledge (of which there are many), none are more striking than our conflicts with Muslims. In the fourteen years since 2001, Muslim terrorists have killed more than a thousand ordinary Europeans, Americans, and Australasians in hotels, buses, railway stations, nightclubs, a theatre, and elsewhere. They've killed many more people of other races.

In this conflict, there is envy and contempt, admiration and derision. There isn't, from our side, discrimination.

We have religious conviction, after all. We're certain that religion is irrelevant to crime, terror, and war.

We remain doggedly determined to keep our Western ideologies: those for which we've decided we fought the Second World redefined War. There are no "we" and "they," only people. Values can't be in conflict, because we insist they're universal. Cultures can't be in conflict, because we're not imposing ours. Civilisations can't be in conflict because our ideologies of inclusion command there be only one civilisation, of which we're all equally part. If we don't believe we're already a unitary world, we think we'd be better off if we were.

There's no postmodern Western Civilisation. We've only ideology and economics. Ours are clashes without civilisation.

We've left lacunas where our countries were. Muslims dream of an Islamic caliphate. We think we're a multicultural caliphate.

Muslims might fight because they seek to conquer. Most races do.

Muslims might fight because they feel insecure, defending their culture much as they defended it in Afghanistan from another anti-national ideology: communism. Our Western world vision raises the spectre of there being no Arab, Persian, or other civilisations much as it obliterates Western Civilisation. Knowing what's becoming of the West surrendering our religion and rest of our cultures in pursuit of multiculturalism, I can't begrudge other races defending theirs.

They're fighting us not in spite of multiculturalism, but because of it. In his 2006 book *Letter to a Christian Nation*, neuroscientist Sam Harris, whose father was a Quaker and mother a Jewess, suggested that religion might be *"the greatest impediment to our building a global civilisation.*" In 2004, he'd published *The End of Faith*. If Muslims aren't fighting Western multiculturalism, they're fighting the end of religion it entails.

In 2012, Sam Mullins, a research fellow at the University of Wollongong's Centre for Transnational Crime Prevention, believed a common theme among Muslim terrorists was their belief that Islam and Muslims were under attack. They must come to the rescue. Theirs are senses of god, peoples, and civilisations akin to those leading our forebears to die on our behalf.

"One of the major differences between crime and terrorism is that terrorism is motivated by altruism," said Australian Federal Police assistant commissioner Steve Lancaster, after joint police and Australian Security and Intelligence Organisation operations Pendennis and Neath through the preceding six years led to twenty-one violent Muslims being convicted and jailed. "They see themselves as freedom fighters and protectors of the wider community. They are Robin Hoods, doing all this dirty work and sacrificing to help other people." Those people are Muslim.

The latest aspiring terrorists in Sydney (Wissam Mahmoud Fattal, Saney Edow Aweys, and Nayev El Sayed) were motivated in part by the gaoling of the previous eighteen in Melbourne; Muslim terror is unending. Along with the thousands of guns and bomb-making materials, police found more than three terabytes of violent Muslim material in their common library, amounting to almost nine hundred million pages.

No terrorists' rant or rationale is in abstract; mere ideologies don't motivate them as they motivate us. They might hate liberty and democracy, fashion and music, but needn't kill us because we don't. They kill us, because they want to kill us.

War is personal. We're not.

Muslims might hate us, but don't need to hate us to value their own. I see more contempt for us than enmity, but given the contempt we feel for our cultures and race, I see where they got it. They call us infidels and, nowadays, they're right. They treat us with contempt no worse than we treat ourselves.

5. LOSING THEIR RELIGION

The perpetrators of the September 2001 attacks saw themselves as being at war with America. America didn't. President George W. Bush (who promptly attended a mosque afterwards in support of Muslims) accused the terrorists of waging war against freedom.

It was much like our redefinition of World War II to have been against fascism instead of Germany and Japan. Ours is a world without enemies; there are only people like us. Bush's war on terror was a war without enemies, as was our subsequent talk of war against extremism. Our world and wars are ideological, without trace of race, religion, or people at all.

Like other wars, we dispense with the truth, compromising the morality of peacetime to pursue our war effort. Within a very short time, we started referring to the attacks not by the attackers but by the date on which they occurred: "nine/eleven," in the American way of numbering dates.

We stopped calling them attacks. In 2004, the makers of the 2002 film *The Bourne Identity* described what happened that day in 2001 as a "tragedy." It sounded accidental.

The 2006 film *World Trade Centre* examined the attacks on those buildings from viewpoints within them, making no mention of the terrorists or Islam. The closing monologue spoke only of the good and evil that human beings do.

We're determined not to let the terrorists win, by which we don't mean defending our races and cultures. We mean maintaining our hospitalities to other races and cultures. We think that to abrogate in any way the generosities we've discovered since the Second World War would mean that we'd lost.

It's an ideological victory in an ideological war: holding fast to what's in our head. We win by losing: losing our countries. We'd lose by winning: saving them. It's the absurdity English writer George Orwell described in his warnings about communism in his 1949 novel *1984*, but it makes perfect sense to us.

Classifying Muslim terror as something other than war does

more to avoid war than everything else we've done. Ours is the war that isn't; it never was. It's a non-war effort. There are still deaths and destruction, but a different moniker.

Terrorism became too judgemental a concept. It's just another crime, and we've long stopped being fussed about crime. If the mindsets of ordinary criminals don't perturb us from constructing them in our global image without race or religion, there's no reason the mindsets of terrorists should. They're more clients to rehabilitate. Crime hadn't impinged upon our ideals, neither would terror.

"As Americans," President Barack Obama said often, including at a Pentagon memorial service in 2010, "we will not and never will be at war with Islam." Nine years had passed since a hundred and eighty-four people were killed there. "It was not a religion that attacked us that September day. It was al-Qaeda, a sorry band of men which perverts religion." I couldn't imagine anyone defending racism, because it had been perverted by Nazis.

By the tenth anniversary of the attacks, it was as if the perpetrators had been characterless spirit beings. (It would be the same with the tenth anniversary of the Bali bombings in 2012.) Only once did I see any of the invisible terrorists mentioned by name. Never was there mention of them being Muslims or Arabs. News reports I read mentioning Muslims talked about the challenges American Muslims had faced since then. Muslims aren't perpetrators, but victims. We don't talk of Germans facing challenges since World War II.

The only other mention I read of Muslims was on the *Huffington Post* website. Human rights attorney Engy Abdelkader claimed that more than forty percent of terrorist attacks foiled since 2001 had been foiled by assistance from Muslims. In our multicultural mind set, Muslims don't commit terrorist attacks. They prevent them.

Other races retain loyalties to their own, as the West no longer comprehends. They report their own to Western authorities before attacks to save those would-be assailants, not us, from harm. They're not so forthcoming *after* attacks.

The penultimate Tuesday morning in March 2016, Muslim Moroccans (including Belgian-born Ibrahim El Bakraoui and Najim Laachraoui who'd attended a Roman Catholic high school and university in Belgium) detonated three nail-bombs at Zaventem airport and Maalbeek metro station in Brussels, killing thirty-two others and injuring more than three hundred. Belgian police said their pleas for help from residents of the Muslim suburbs of Molenbeek and Schaerbeek were ignored. Even those without jihadi sympathies were unlikely to report terrorists to authorities. Muslims treated police with contempt.

The multiculturalist West, not Muslims, decided Islam is a religion of peace, even *the* religion of peace. Without regard for the Koran, we decided it not after years of peace or even a single moment or action of peace, but after years of Islamic crime and terror, most monumentally that morning in September 2001.

More often than not, we call Muslim criminals and terrorists not real Muslims. Reading extracts from the Koran left me thinking that if Mohammed walked the earth today, the West would insist he's not a real Muslim.

Muslims and we might describe militant Muslims as Islamists as if they are somehow not Muslims. It would have been like referring to Nazis as Nazists.

Every right we claim for ourselves, we grant terrorists, except one. We deny them their right to decide their religion. They think they're Muslims. We insist they're not. We reduce their religion to our definition of practices to follow.

Conversely, Muslims drinking alcohol and frequenting prostitutes without committing crimes retain their right to choose their religion. They're Muslims.

The West invented the idea of radical Islam, as against normal, moderate Islam. Only radical Islam might harm us, we said.

"These descriptions are very ugly," retorted Turkey's Prime Minister Recep Tayyip Erdoğan in 2007. "It is offensive and an insult to our religion. There is no moderate or immoderate Islam. Islam is Islam and that's it." We ignored him.

We dismiss Muslim terror with phrases such as "the majority of peace-loving Muslims," even if the only evidence such a majority exists are the Muslim community leaders saying so and our new-found confidence in other races and cultures. Palestinian leaders condemn terrorism with statements in English but not in the language their people speak, Arabic. It's good public relations. We understand public relations.

Evidence otherwise, we dismiss. "*Islam was never a religion of peace,*" insisted Islamic State leader Abu Bakr al-Baghdadi in a message published on various Islamic websites in 2015. "*Islam is the religion of fighting."*

We went from al-Qaeda to Islamic State, but even Islamic State we don't call Islamic. We call it Daesh.

Only the headline changed. The terror did not.

The Centre for Security Policy commissioned a poll in May 2015 revealing that fifty-one percent of American Muslims wanted a sharia court system outside the American legal system. Almost a quarter believed establishing sharia justified violent jihad. A minority can be big.

We don't treat the crimes of our past so particularly. No lamenting of Western history is tempered with reference to the majority of peace-loving Christians.

We're accommodating Islam as we've never before accommodated the beliefs of people attacking us, not even communism during the Cold War. *"We did not say the Soviet system was morally equivalent to ours,"* wrote Somali-born Ayaan Hirsi Ali in her 2015 book *Heretic*, identifying with the West rather than the Islam she'd renounced. *"Nor did we proclaim that Soviet communism was an ideology of peace."* When people say they're killing in the name of Islam, she said we should believe them.

We distinguish Muslim extremists from other Muslims, although the only distinction seems to be that extremists are terrorists. We don't distinguish white racist extremists from other racists, or fascist extremists from other fascists.

Much like radical or fundamentalist Muslims, or indeed those of any other religion, there is no extremist Islam. There is only Islam, with its competing denominations.

Some Muslims are devout. Some are not. The criminals and terrorists do not seem disproportionately devout or disproportionately not.

We link the Holocaust with our past racial and religious prejudices, but refuse to link Muslim terrorism with Islam. Most Muslims going about their ordinary days aren't trying to kill anyone, but neither were most Germans before or during World War II. There's no defence for the majority of peace-loving Germans, let alone the majority of peace-loving Nazis.

Muslim terrorists make no efforts to negotiate peace like Adolf Hitler's deputy Rudolf Hess flying to Britain in 1941. The British arrested Hess and imprisoned him for the rest of his life. Most Nazis wanted neither war nor the genocide upon which Hitler embarked. (They weren't the reason I joked glibly through my undergraduate years about a mythical organisation: Nazis for Peace.) We stopped searching for peace with Germany in 1939 and Serbia in 1999, but keep insisting we're at peace with Muslims. We didn't think of sitting down with Macedonians in 2001 trying to understand their grievances.

An Australian news report the middle Thursday of July 2009 mentioned the risk of terrorism in Indonesia from Jemaah Islamiyah, describing the organisation only as being Indonesian. In case the name gave anything away, all but one reference abbreviated it to the innocuous initials JI, which sounded more like a friend's nickname or music shop than anything sinister.

The following day, terrorist bombs in Djakarta killed nine people at the Ritz-Carlton Hotel, including a New Zealand businessman. News reports spoke of al-Qaeda but not Muslims, with just a single reference I saw to Indonesia being *"a mainly Muslim country."*

Also that day, eighteen-year-old Dani Dwi Permana walked into a meeting of executives at the JW Marriott Hotel in Djakarta and detonated two bombs, murdering three Australians and two others. Writing for the *Sydney Morning Herald* newspaper, Tom Allard described Permana as *"nice, but...easily led."* He was a multiple murderer, but a nice multiple murderer. If we contemplated the same of Europeans, then we'd see Nazi storm troopers as nice, but easily led.

So kind was Allard's description of the basketball-loving boy he called Dani, I could've thought Dani was being nominated for a citizenship award. When quoting the school friend who said he talked freely of waging jihad, Allard defined jihad as being *"the Islamic notion of struggle that is typically a peaceful pursuit by the devout but is twisted by terrorist groups to justify mass murder."*

Hitler's book *Mein Kampf* translates roughly as *My Struggle*, thus *My Jihad*. I couldn't imagine Allard saying racism was a peaceful pursuit by the good, which Hitler twisted to justify mass murder.

The Koran calls upon Muslims to carry out jihad. Whether jihad means internal struggle, external violence, or both, it lacks peace and contentment. Arid Uka was a Kosovar who grew up in Frankfurt and worked at the airport. His "personal jihad" was shooting at a bus filled with young American soldiers in March 2011, killing two.

Jihadists became another euphemism we use to distinguish Muslim killers from other Muslims. The great thing about that euphemism is that they don't need to be Muslim.

American commentator Justin Rosario called Scott Roeder a Christian jihadist, after Roeder murdered physician George Tiller (an usher at the Reformation Lutheran Church in Wichita) in 2009 because Tiller performed late-term abortions. Roeder wasn't a churchgoer and seems not to have called himself a Christian, but that didn't matter. We did. Muslim jihadists are simply jihadists, while white people with no thought of Christianity or jihad are Christian jihadists. Christianity becomes like Islam, in matters of murder.

Still, even a word like "jihadist" has too many connotations with Islam. It gives too much away.

News reports of five men convicted in February 2010 of preparing terrorist acts in Sydney referred only to them being "*zealots*," much like the zealots who ban cigarette smoking in public places or demand their children wear seatbelts. These zealots happened to want to detonate explosives. They were among nine men arrested, all of whose names the law suppressed from publication.

Part way through the article, mention was made that the men wanted to carry out "*violent jihad so as to coerce the Australian government to change its policies regarding the invasion of Muslim countries.*" Still, describing the would-be terrorists as Muslim would've been distasteful. "*The five accused wore traditional clothing and four of them wore prayer caps.*" I'm certain those traditions and caps weren't Western.

"*During the judge's summing up, some of them smiled and, during breaks in his address, some of them exchanged pleasantries with each other. After the sentences were pronounced and the judge left the bench, all five broke into smiles. Two men shouted from the back of the court in Arabic: 'Be patient. Allah is with you.'*"

Allah certainly seemed to be. Religion isn't in play, not for the West, however much Muslims think it is.

Rather than mentioning their race or religion, we identify terrorists by the scenes of their attacks. When ten men murdered a hundred and sixty-six people through three days of terror in Mumbai, beginning the last Wednesday of November 2008, Western media made little mention they were Muslim Pakistanis. They were the Mumbai bombers, until rumour came that some might've been British born or British citizens. Suddenly, we had no hesitation describing them. They were British. Not merely British citizens or British-born people of Pakistani origin, they were British.

As it turned out, the rumour was wrong. They were again the Mumbai bombers.

While we believe Britons and Americans can be of any race or religion, other races don't. The only Mumbai terrorist captured alive, after pretending to be dead, was Mohammed Ajmal Amir Kasab. He said they'd been told to "target whites, preferably Americans and British." They had a special place for the Jews, the Nariman Building cultural centre, where they tortured six before executing them.

None of it deterred commentator Greg Barns, a few days after the Mumbai attack, from lambasting Australians merely for protesting plans by a Brisbane Muslim school to build another Muslim school on the Gold Coast. "*If you needed any confirmation that Australia's xenophobic and racist underbelly is still alive and well,*" he wrote on the first day of December, Advent, "*then look no further than Queensland's Gold Coast.*"

I'd met Greg several times when I worked for Otter Gold Mines Limited and he was chief executive of the Australian Gold Council. He was a tall man, dedicated to his work, but the passion he felt for gold was much less than he found promoting the interests of Muslims, while living in quiet, serene Hobart, dependent (as we are) upon websites.

The Muslim school condemned the protesters as un-Australian, although a few months earlier it fired a teacher, Pravin Chand, for "not fitting in with the school's ethos." Chand wanted to play the Australian national anthem, which the school considered against the "Islamic view and ethos." Greg didn't respond, but I imagined him seething at the newspaper for publishing Chand's claims, the words of another teacher confirming them, and a memorandum to staff that "*the singing of the anthem will be put on hold.*" The school denied the allegations.

Greg moved on. Monday, a week later, he criticised the severity of a gaol sentence handed down by a Queensland court to a schoolmistress convicted of having a two-year sexual relationship with a fourteen-year-old schoolgirl already suffering eating and behavioural problems. It was interesting to imagine how a Muslim school, let alone a Muslim court, would've treated the lesbian woman and girl. White people only criticise each other.

We're so different to other races. Only we separate justice from people, our people.

Indians have nationalism. Instead of Western ethics, Indian lawyers have morality. They said representing the surviving gunman who'd killed their countrymen in Mumbai would've been immoral.

The West refuses to imagine a war under way, but Kasab believed he was "a hero and a patriotic Pakistani at war," said the Supreme Court of India. He was hanged after being convicted of eighty-six offences, including waging war against India.

The Mumbai bombing wasn't a problem for us. It was something to admire.

When Australian television broadcast the 2011 American documentary *A Perfect Terrorist*, the television guide burst forth with admiration. "*It has been called the most spectacular terror attack since 9/11. On November 26, 2008, 10 men from a Pakistani militant group launched an assault on Mumbai that left 166 dead. Later, India learned that one of the militants had been casing the city for two years, developing a blueprint for terror. His name was David Coleman Headley and he was an American citizen. This documentary investigates the mysterious circumstances behind Headley's rise from heroin dealer and US government informant to master plotter of the 2008 attack on Mumbai.*"

With such veneration, it could hardly have hurt to mention David Coleman Headley wasn't always his name. He was born Daood Sayed Gilani in Washington, where his father was a Pakistani diplomat. He'd changed his name to make border crossings easier. It obviously worked.

6. STAVING OFF PREJUDICE

Wars often require all of a country's resources, but our primary response to Muslim terror hasn't been military. Nor has it involved the police. It hasn't involved curtailing immigration or winding back multiculturalism. (By 2010, Islam had become the second most common religion in twenty American states.) Where our forebears spoke of eternal vigilance in terms of armed forces, we see it in terms of political will: to ensure people don't look less favourably upon Muslims.

Among the new words Islamic terrorism brought is so-called Islamophobia: a fear or disliking of Muslims. We label people expressing any concern about rapidly growing Muslim populations as Islamophobes. Funnily enough, Islamisation seems only to appear in quotation marks, "Islamisation," as if there could never be such a thing. We'll be happily multicultural forever.

Not welcoming life under sharia would be Islamophobia.

There are no quotation marks for Islamophobia. Akin to other phobias, we insist it can only be irrational.

Never was there a crueller, more oppressive word than Islamophobia. The country most accused of Islamophobia is France. She has admitted more Muslim immigrants than any other.

Islamophobia is another slander to silence dissent. Salman Ramadan Abedi was born in Manchester to a family of Libyan-born refugees. An observer warning a British policeman about Abedi before an Ariana Grande concert in the Manchester Arena on the fourth Monday in May 2017 was reputedly rebuked by the policeman for Islamophobia.

Christopher Wild was suspicious of the man he saw with a rucksack, apparently hiding, on a mezzanine floor. "It's a kids' concert," his girlfriend Julie Whitley said to him. "Why should he be sat there with a massive rucksack out of sight of everyone? It's just very strange."

Wild reported his concerns to a security guard, who fobbed him off. He said to Wild that "he already knew about him. That was about it, really." The security guard was Mohammed Agha.

Standing ten or fifteen feet away, eighteen-year-old security guard Kyle Lawler also had a "bad feeling" about Abedi. Lawler did not approach him for fear of being branded a racist.

Shortly afterwards, Abedi detonated his bomb. He murdered twenty-two concertgoers and their parents waiting to collect them afterwards. He wounded eight hundred, including children.

American singer Ariana Grande insisted afterwards that people should not be afraid. We weren't.

The following month, on the first Saturday in June 2017, Londoners hid under restaurant tables during another terror attack. A mobile telephone in one restaurant recorded someone insisting: "It's not the Muslims."

It was the Muslims. Pakistan-born British citizen Khuram Shazad Butt, North African asylum-seeker Rachid Redouane, and Youssef Zaghba (born to a Muslim Moroccan father and a Roman Catholic Italian mother who converted to Islam when they married) murdered eight people and injured forty-eight in London that night. "This is for Allah," they screamed as they did.

The only real Islamophobia is the West's irrational fear of linking Muslims and Islam with anything bad. We don't discriminate between religions, whatever the evidence we should.

Nor do we discriminate one religious prejudice from another. *"For some time it has been clear that Islamophobia is a contemporary form of anti-Jewish prejudice,"* wrote Guy Rundle for the *Crikey* daily mail in March 2012. Muslims are the Jews of our time; we lump them together as victims.

Rundle was reporting on the murders of three Jewish children and a rabbi at a school in Toulouse, shortly after the murders of three French North African paratroopers by the same gunman. Without any suspects or motives identified, Sydney's *MX* commuter magazine reported suspicions the gunman was a Nazi. The only bases for those suspicions were the victims' races, but we only conceived white people being prejudiced.

We link white racism, not Islam, to crime. We collectively blame white people, not Muslims, for terror. Rundle blamed French prejudice and particularly President Nicholas Sarkozy who, in the course of an election campaign, had said there were "too many immigrants in France."

In Rundle's words, *"a violent xenophobia is off the leash in France."*

The murderer was not a Nazi. He was Mohammed Merah. His mother was Algerian.

News reports didn't call Merah a Muslim. He was a jihadist, motivated by France banning the full Islamic veil as well as French military actions against Muslims. We excused him.

Conversely, two of his three paratrooper victims were readily identified as Muslims. I thus read for the first time of Muslims considering Muslims in Western armies to be traitors. I haven't read that again; it hardly suits our vision of the world, we Islamophiles.

Muslims don't equate Islamophobia to anti-Semitism. "*O, you who believe!*" the Koran, surah 5, verse 51 tells them, "*do not take the Jews and the Christians for friends; they are friends of each other; and whoever amongst you takes them for a friend, then surely he is one of them; surely Allah does not guide the unjust people.*"

Egyptian Nonie Darwish was born a Muslim in 1949. She converted to Christianity after moving to America in 1978. In her 2008 book *Cruel and Usual Punishment: The Terrifying Global Implications of Islamic Law*, she said there are thirty-five thousand, two hundred and thirteen Koran verses, hadiths, Muslim scriptures, and other sharia commanding or encouraging violence, war, annihilation, corporal punishment, hatred, boycott, humiliation, and subjugation, primarily of non-Muslims.

We're not worried about Muslim prejudices. We worry about ours.

After the Paris terrorist attacks of November 2015, American presidential candidate Donald Trump said American should develop a national database of Muslims living in the country to protect people from terrorism. "What else can you compare this to except to pre-war Nazi Germany?" asked Ibrahim Hooper, national spokesman for the Council on American–Islamic Relations. "There's no other comparison..."

Rabbi Jack Moline drew the same conclusion. House of Representatives speaker Paul Ryan later described the idea as something the Gestapo would do, referring to Nazi Germany's secret state police.

The first Wednesday in December 2015, Islamic State sympathisers American-born Syed Rizwan Farook and his wife Tashfeen Malik murdered fourteen people at a Department of Public Health training event and holiday party in California. Trump thus proposed a ban on Muslims entering America until "*our country's representatives can figure out what is going on*," in the words of a campaign press release. (Exemptions from the ban would include American citizens.)

Another barrage of bipartisan condemnation followed. Democratic Party presidential candidate Martin O'Malley, a former governor of Maryland, called Trump "*a fascist demagogue.*"

In our continuing war against fascism, our enemies aren't Muslim. They aren't Arab, African, or Albanian. They're white.

Bastille Day 2016, President François Hollande declared France's greatest threat to be not Islam but French populism: nationalism. A few hours later, driving a truck, Tunisian-born Mohamed Lahouaiej-Bouhlel mowed down crowds on the *Promenade des Anglais*, killing eighty-six and injuring more than three hundred. "*Allahu Akbar!*" he shouted.

Prime Minister Manuel Valls was more tolerant than he'd been of nationalism. He said "times have changed, and France is going to have to live with terrorism."

No number of Muslim terrorists (like no number of other criminals) convinces us to worry about anything but white people's prejudice. We feel the world and our lives are most under threat not from other races or religions, but from the West slipping back into prejudice. We're extraordinarily arrogant about white people's power and dismissive of other people's power to harm us, but we remember the Holocaust. Arrogance kicks us in our guts every day of our lives.

We defend Muslims because we defend everyone from white people. We refuse to link race or religion to crime and terror, because that's what Nazis did. To be wary of Muslims might legitimise Hitler's wariness of Jews, we worry; we're only wary of white people. Hitler made negative generalisations about other races and religions, and we aren't going to raise even the smallest spectre of such generalisations being true, for fear of where they ended. The Holocaust remains the most profound incident of racial and religious profiling in Western history, never to be repeated.

Other races and religions harming us don't justify us discriminating. Nazis feared Jews harming Germany.

Having opened our borders to all, we can't close them to Muslims but not others. Reinstating discrimination against particular races or religions would smack of the Nazis zeroing in upon Jews. Considering the possibility that discrimination against Muslims is reasonable would be like considering the possibility that anti-Semitism was reasonable, we think, which would be to consider the possibility the Holocaust was reasonable.

Australian and Victorian governments financed the Muslim Emergency Management Plan, devised by the Islamic Council of Victoria with support from the Department of Premier and Cabinet's Office of Multicultural Affairs and Citizenship, launched in 2011. The plan focussed on hate crimes, but not Muslims killing people. It feared people being rude to Muslims.

Islamic Council general manager Nail Aykan said a Muslim terrorist attack would undoubtedly cause a backlash against Muslims. Police attention would focus upon not the attack but the backlash. The "prejudice-motivated crime strategy" encompassed crimes linked to race, religion, sex, age, disability, or homelessness, but not those of the criminals. Police weren't asked to develop data based on a criminal's race or religion, but on crime motivated by the victim's race or religion, just as the Holocaust was.

Muslim terror makes us manage the Christians. We work hardest to answer not an enemy's terror, but the fears of our friends.

The United Nations Committee on the Elimination of Racial Discrimination didn't care about crime committed by immigrants and foreigners in America. It investigated eight hundred allegations of racially motivated mistreatment of them from 2001 to '08. Concerned about racial and religious profiling of Arabs, Muslims, and South Asians in America's response to terrorism, it inspected America in May 2008.

After a Christmas 2009 attempted suicide bombing, America restricted travel for citizens of fourteen countries, thirteen of which were primarily Muslim. "Religious intolerance is the new racism," complained Minority Rights Group International director Mark Lattimer. "Many communities that have faced racial discrimination for decades are now being targeted because of their religion." We're not to counter Muslim terrorism with thought of religion.

In a July 2010 report, Minority Rights Group International accused Europe and America of persecuting Muslims because counterterrorism measures disproportionately affected Muslims. Meanwhile, Muslim persecution of Christians in Iraq and Pakistan included killings, torture, forcible conversions to Islam, and burning churches.

The report was particularly concerned about the Swiss, who'd avoided two world wars in their chalets in ski passes. There'd never been a Swiss empire, but Switzerland accepting refugees in recent years meant Muslims had grown rapidly to number almost five percent of the population. After three mosques were built and a fourth was planned, rebellious Swiss set up a referendum to ban not mosques, but merely minarets: the militaristic observation points towering over surrounding streets.

Christian, Jewish, and Muslim leaders came together to oppose even that feeble assertion of Swiss sovereignty. Jews were particularly irate, regarding the proposed ban as reflecting "extremist ideas" (in the same league, presumably, as Nazism) and a threat to Swiss religious harmony. Unwilling to defend Western cultures, harmony depends upon us granting other religions everything they want.

Nobody imagined Muslim gratitude to Switzerland for admitting those refugees. There was only jihad, after the Swiss narrowly passed the minaret ban.

"It is against unbelieving and apostate Switzerland that jihad ought to be proclaimed by all means," said Libyan leader Muammar Gaddafi to thousands of Muslims marking Mohammed's birthday in the Mediterranean coastal city of Benghazi in February 2010, broadcast on Libyan television. "Jihad against Switzerland, against Zionism, against foreign aggression is not terrorism. Any Muslim around the world who has dealings with Switzerland is an infidel against Islam, against Mohammed, against God, against the Koran."

At the time, Gaddafi was our friend. Just as well.

We'd forgotten Gaddafi had been a pariah for killing Western people. He'd become a pariah again, for killing Libyans.

While any hesitation to wrap our arms around Muslims makes us guilty of Islamophobia, public railing against America, Europe, or the entire West doesn't make Muslims guilty of Ameriphobia, Europophobia, or Westophobia. Those words don't exist. I made them up. There's no Christophobia because we think fearing or disliking Christians is perfectly rational, even sensible. Never has there been an era for creating words like ours, but decades of crime and terror haven't allowed us words disparaging of other races or religions.

Kenya was celebrating the International Day of Peace one Saturday in September 2013, when men we called simply attackers seized control of the Westgate shopping mall, Nairobi, at midday. At least sixty-seven people, including an eight-month-pregnant woman and a five-year-old child, died in the carnage. This was no indiscriminate slaughter, and not simply because the killers chose a mall popular with Westerners. "The gunmen told Muslims to stand up and leave," said shopper Elijah Kamau. "They were safe, and non-Muslims would be targeted."

Not trusting people claiming to be Muslims, the attackers thrust rifles in their faces, forcing them to answer a death test. "I hid under a car with my daughters," said information technology engineer Charles Karani, "and I saw the men line up maybe forty people and ask them who was Muslim and if they were to prove it by saying the name of the prophet's mother. Those who got it wrong were shot."

"If they had found me…," said New Zealander Greg Aldous, who hid in a box, "I'm white, so I'm dead. They're not even going to think twice. They hate your skin colour." No *Australian Broadcasting Corporation News* report I read mentioned the gunmen's discrimination.

The *News Limited Network* merely described as *"religiously motivated"* two suicide bombers killing eighty-five worshippers in the All Saints' Church in Peshawar, Pakistan, the following day. Simply being Christian in a Muslim country can provoke a Muslim response.

Two weeks later, on the first Saturday of October, *Sydney Morning Herald* television broadcast a Vanguard documentary *Islamophobia*. It reported a rise of attacks *upon* Muslims, amid growing religious tensions worldwide since 2001.

Omar Al-Kutobi arrived in Australia in 2009, was granted a protection visa, and obtained Australian citizenship in 2013. Mohammad Kiad was granted a visa under the family and spousal visa arrangements. Both received Australian government welfare payments of Newstart allowances. Nevertheless, in February 2015, they knelt before an Islamic State flag in suburban Sydney and pledged: "I swear to almighty Allah we will carry out the first operation for the soldiers of the caliphate in Australia. I swear to almighty Allah, blond people, there is no room for blame between you and us. We only are you, stabbing the kidneys and striking the necks."

Other races discriminate. We don't.

The first news report I saw mentioning Muslims in Australian gaols was in 2010. Setting the scene for a story about serial killer Ivan Milat, Chris Masters reported that the High Risk Management Unit at Goulburn Correctional Centre "*opened in the same year the World Trade Centre was destroyed, is home to seventeen Muslim inmates, nine convicted of terrorism offences. The sound of daily prayer now mingles with the clash of bolts and hum of air-conditioning… On the day we visit, so does an imam.*" Milat wasn't Muslim.

In 2007, maximum security prisons in Terre Haute, Indiana and Marion, Illinois secretly opened Communication Management Units, where authorities monitored prisoners' every communication with the outside world. In March 2011, American Bureau of Prisons spokeswoman Tracy Billingsley couldn't state the proportion of Muslims among the seventy-one prisoners, insisting "it is irrelevant."

Other sources suggested that between sixty-five and seventy-two percent of the hundred prisoners who'd been in those units were Muslim. With our rejection of religious discrimination, that wasn't reason to fear Muslims. It was evidence of discrimination.

"So, that's a tenfold over-representation," complained Alexis Agathocleous, attorney at the Centre for Constitutional Rights; six percent of prisoners in American gaols were Muslim. "That obviously raises concerns about religious profiling." He also complained there was "a pattern of people with unpopular political beliefs," whatever that meant, "being designated to the C.M.U."

Our dogged opposition to religious discrimination means we're unwilling to deal with threats grounded in religion, without dealing with everyone. Past allegations of discrimination had led prison officials to confine prisoners in the Communication Management Units because they *weren't* Muslim. Guards called them "balancers."

To prove we're not prejudiced, our war on terror is an equal opportunity war. When the threats posed by some Muslim leaders made the Home Office ban them from entering Britain from 2005, it also banned non-Muslims. "*We will want to ensure that the names disclosed reflect the broad range of cases,*" said a British government document, "*and are not all Islamic extremists.*" Had the Second World War been fought on the same basis, we'd have bombed Cornwall each time we bombed Germany.

7. ABANDONING THE VULNERABLE

In Australia, it's become fashionable to equate the division between Christianity and Islam with that between Protestantism and Roman Catholicism before the 1960s. Whatever else might be said of our past, we could walk along whatever streets in our cities we wanted without feeling alien or afraid.

Similarly, the West equates Islamic terror with Irish Republican terror of the past, but the latter didn't claim to act in the name of God. Other Roman Catholics weren't involved.

Irish Republicanism was Irish, not Roman Catholic, nationalism. Its objective was uniting All Ireland, not destroying England. We judged Irish nationalism, even Irish, having regard to everything Irish did.

Nobody denied the sympathies and even support of Roman Catholic areas of Northern Ireland for the terrorists. We refuse to acknowledge Muslim sympathy and support for Islamic terror.

"When will you journalists realise that it is deeply rooted in Islam's culture to rape and brutalize women who refuse to comply with Islamic teachings," wrote Michael Hess, a Swedish politician who'd lived in Muslim countries, after so many women were raped in Cairo's Tahrir Square during the Arab Spring of 2011. *"There is a strong connection between rapes in Sweden and the number of immigrants from"* the Middle East and North Africa.

Hess delivered statistical evidence at his trial in 2014 to support his claims, but was nevertheless convicted of denigrating ethnic groups, fined, and given a suspended jail sentence. "The court notes that the question of whether or not Michael Hess' pronouncement is true, or appeared to be true to Michael Hess, has no bearing on the case."

The truth is irrelevant in the multiculturalist West. What matters is not denigrating other races or religions.

We're certain religion is irrelevant to people of other races being criminals or terrorists. It's relevant only to excuse them.

In Britain, the cases against Somali sisters Ambaro, Ayan, and Hibo Maxamed and their cousin Ifrah Nur turned on them being Muslims, but only in their defence. On the penultimate Friday of June 2010, young British care worker Rhea Page approached a taxi rank in the Leicester city centre with her boyfriend, when the four Somalis began calling her a "white bitch" and a "white slag." One grabbed her hair and threw her to the ground, where the Somalis took turns to kick her repeatedly. "Kill the white slag," they screamed, ripping out clumps of her hair, bruising and grazing her head, back, legs, and arms.

Page required hospital treatment. Her repeated absences from work suffering stress, panic attacks, and flashbacks led to her losing her job. Seventeen months later, she was still undergoing counselling, but the Leicester Crown Court didn't send the four Somalis to gaol. Judge Robert Brown gave them only suspended sentences because, being Muslims, they were "not used to being drunk."

He also thought the women might've felt Page's boyfriend, Lewis Moore, used unreasonable force in trying desperately to defend her from attack. He presumably should've politely asked the Somalis to leave her alone, failing which he should have left her to them.

When the West turned against our racial and religious loyalties, we betrayed most of all our poor and vulnerable. Abid Siddique and Mohammed Liaqat were devout Muslim family men, but that was within their South Asian community. Outside, they cruised the streets of Derby, England in a silver B.M.W. 5 series car they called their "Rape Rover," stopping to chat and flirt with white girls aged between twelve and fifteen on the street they saw as being vulnerable. They offered the girls cigarettes, vodka, and cocaine to secure their mobile telephone numbers. Later, they invited them to parties at which they abused the girls, passing them around their gang of thirteen men and those men's relatives, filming them on their mobile telephones for more friends' gratification. Their systematic sexual abuse continued for a year and a half.

Their conviction and gaoling in 2011 depended upon a *Times* newspaper investigation of Pakistani men across the north of England and Midlands sexually exploiting predominantly white girls. Police Operation Retriever identified twenty-eight victims aged between twelve and eighteen. Officers believed many more victims didn't come forward.

It turned out police had previously identified a series of such cases since the 1990s, but there'd been what Melanie Phillips writing in the *Daily Mail* newspaper called "*a conspiracy of silence over this phenomenon.*" Grooming them for sex, groups of Muslim men gave alcohol and drugs to hundreds of white girls aged primarily between eleven and sixteen, predominantly from troubled backgrounds, craving attention from absent parents. The men abducted, raped or otherwise sexually assaulted, and enslaved them.

Morality is tribal. A Muslim man explained that white girls were targeted because "if they did it to a Muslim girl, they'd be shot."

"These people think that white girls have fewer morals," elaborated Mohammed Shafiq, chief executive of the national Muslim youth organisation, the Ramadhan Foundation, "and are less valuable than our girls."

Muslims heavily populated the Blackburn constituency. Parliamentarian Jack Straw said some British Pakistani men plied emotionally vulnerable white girls with gifts and drugs, regarding them as "easy meat."

Home Affairs Select Committee chairman Keith Vaz called Straw's comments "pretty dangerous." (They were more dangerous, it seems, than Muslim men raping white girls.)

Others accused Straw of being inflammatory and stereotyping the British Muslim community. (We accepted stereotyping white girls.)

Life was no better for poor English girls in Rochdale, a large market town in Greater Manchester. Few towns could claim a longer English heritage than Rochdale, which the Domesday Book of 1086 recorded under Recedham Manor. In multicultural England, that didn't matter.

From 2002, Greater Manchester Police were aware of close to fifty Muslim Asian men picking out girls in Rochdale for being white, vulnerable, and under age. They plied them with alcohol, food, and small sums of money in return for sexual acts. A thirteen-year-old victim became pregnant and had the child aborted. Another was forced to have sex with twenty men in one night.

In 2005, a sexual health adviser detailed the kidnap and rape of underage Miss F. "*8.30am yesterday three men she did not know took her to a hotel. She presented at the Crisis Intervention Team with love bites and acute abdominal pain. She was found accommodation at Night Stop but continued to have abdominal pain and went to A & E. She was escorted away by three Asian men before she was seen. She is now missing."* Miss F *"is believed to be using substances to the extent that she does not know what she is doing. A couple of days ago, wearing a sari, she was carried across the road by three Asian men. She was obviously under the influence of some substance. She has no memory of what happened at the hotel."*

The report was forwarded to the social services and crisis intervention teams at Crossfield Mill. Miss F's mother gave police and social workers the names and nicknames of more than a dozen men who'd abused her daughter and who she feared would abuse her other two daughters, but authorities wouldn't intervene. "I wanted the three of them to be put into child protection but they wouldn't do it," Miss F's mother told the Liverpool Crown Court in 2012. "I must have called in to social services eight or nine times and phoned them lots of times. A police officer did tell me, and a social worker has told me since, that they're frightened to do anything with the Asians because they might be accused of being racist against them." The Asian men went onto abuse her other two daughters, too.

In August 2008, fifteen-year-old Girl A cried for help during a six-hour-long police interview. She gave details of her abusers and where the attacks occurred. She handed officers underwear that proved she'd been raped by two men in a single attack. Nevertheless, the Crown Prosecution Service twice decided not to prosecute her attackers.

The abuse continued. At its worst, Girl A was being driven to flats and houses to be raped by up to five men a night, four or five days a week. Her ordeal ended when she fell pregnant and her teachers became concerned by the number of Asian men picking her up from school. They forced social workers to intervene.

Sure enough, when the police investigation into the assaults finally began, Asians accused the police of racism. Kabeer Hassan, Abdul Aziz, Abdul Rauf, Mohammed Sajid, Adil Khan, Abdul Qayyum, Mohammed Amin, Hamid Safi, and a fifteen-year-old boy who couldn't be named for legal reasons continued claiming to be the victims of police racism when they appeared before the Liverpool Crown Court in 2012, accused of running a child exploitation ring in Rochdale.

"All of you treated" the victims "as though they were worthless and beyond any respect," Judge Gerald Clifton told the Afghans and Pakistanis. "One of the factors leading to that was the fact that they were not part of your community or religion. Some of you, when arrested, said it was triggered by race. That is nonsense. What triggered this prosecution was your lust and greed. In some cases those girls were raped callously, viciously and violently."

"They were petrified of being called racist," explained Ann Cryer, former parliamentarian for Keighley, of the police and social services, "and so reverted to the default of political correctness."

Not only are we aggressively accusing each other of racism. We're determinedly defending ourselves from accusations of racism, no matter who suffers.

Assistant chief constable Steve Heywood denied officers were reluctant to confront the issue of race, by insisting race was irrelevant anyway. "It just happens that they are Asian men," he insisted. (The men thought race was relevant, when picking their victims.)

Poor white girls fared even worse in Rotherham, South Yorkshire, where the Rotherham Labour Party convened Asian-only meetings because Asians did not want to mix with white people. Only white people fear being accused of racism.

Police largely ignored allegations of gangs of principally Pakistani men sexually abusing white girls as young as eleven since 1997. Previously confidential documents seen by the *Times* newspaper in 2012 revealed evidence of thousands of crimes, including an Iraqi Kurd asylum seeker and four Pakistanis forcing a fourteen-year-old girl to perform sex acts on them.

When police didn't ignore the girls' plight, they prosecuted *them*. A *"large group of adult males"* plied a thirteen-year-old girl with vodka intoxicating her, but weren't prosecuted when the girl was found with them in a derelict house at three o'clock in the morning. She was arrested for a public order offence.

Police arrested a British Pakistani man found in a car with a bottle of vodka and a twelve-year-old British girl, but only on suspicion of stealing the car. She was also arrested. Police didn't charge him in relation to the pornographic images of the girl on his telephone.

Police found a fourteen-year-old girl missing for a week in a car under the influence of drugs with a man twenty years older than she was. He'd sexually abused her, but was arrested only for drug possession.

Police were aware of *"networks of Asian males exploiting young white females,"* trafficking victims to cities including Bristol, Manchester, and Birmingham. The Home Office funded research reporting in 2002 that officers treated the young victims as *"deviant and promiscuous"* while *"the men they were found with were never questioned or investigated."* Just twice were groups of men prosecuted for sexual abuse in South Yorkshire from 1996 to 2012.

Rotherham Metropolitan Borough Council concealed racial links in the crimes because they had *"cultural characteristics...which are locally sensitive in terms of diversity,"* according to a 2010 report from the Rotherham Safeguarding Children Board. It warned of *"sensitivities of ethnicity with potential to endanger the harmony of community relationships."* The council responded to one white girl sexually abused since the age of twelve by offering her classes in Urdu and Punjabi.

An inquiry conducted by academic Alexis Jay reported in 2014 a collective failure by the police and the children's services department at Rotherham Council to deal with at least fourteen hundred cases between 1997 and 2013. The children "were raped by multiple perpetrators, they were trafficked to other towns and cities in the north of England. They were abducted, beaten, and intimidated," she said. "There were examples of children being doused with petrol and threatened with being set alight. They were threatened with guns, made to witness brutally violent rapes and threatened they would be the next if they told anyone."

Victims described the majority of abusers as Asian men. Council staff feared being labelled racist if they responded.

After suffering bullying and being diagnosed with learning difficulties, Laura Wilson was placed on the child protection register at the age of eleven and sent to a special school. Social services in Rotherham knew she was at risk of being groomed for sex by Pakistani men, but fifteen different agencies failed to become involved. At sixteen, her boyfriend was Ashtiaq Asghar, but she fell pregnant to his friend Ishaq Hussain and told Asghar's relatives about her two affairs. In October 2010, when she was seventeen years old, Asghar lured her to a secluded canal in Rotherham. He stabbed her repeatedly in the head with a knife, leaving her dying in the water.

"I honestly think it was an honour killing for putting shame on the family," said Wilson's mother Margaret. "They needed to shut Laura up and they did."

"Few services actually saw, observed and heard" Wilson *"as the highly vulnerable child she was and whom society had a responsibility to protect,"* said a serious case review into the murder carried out by academic Pat Cantrill. "There was a consistently high threshold before concern triggered action," she said, "and my view is that the attitude of the professional culture was, overall, too tolerant."

It didn't end. From 2006 until '12 in Aylesbury, Vikram Singh, Asif Hussain, Arshad Jani, Mohammed Imran, Akbari Kha, and Taimoor Khan prostituted two vulnerable white girls desperate for love. One was passed around almost on a daily basis from the age of thirteen until she was sixteen for sex with sixty or seventy men, almost all of them Asian. "If they pursued Asian under-age girls," said Judge John Bevan Q.C., "they would have paid a heavy price in their community."

White girls aren't the only victims in multicultural Britain. In 2007, the Hindu Forum of Britain said hundreds of Hindu and Sikh girls had been intimidated by Muslim men taking them on dates and terrorising them until they converted to Islam. The Sikh Media Monitoring group described *"the deliberate and targeted sexual degradation of Sikh women purely because of their religion"* and a minority of young Muslim men boasting about *"seducing the Kaffir women."*

Kaffir is Arabic slang derogating non-Muslims. We didn't know which way to turn.

If religious pluralism fails, then multiculturalism fails, as happened with Jews and Christians in Europe. We persevere with Muslims because Nazi Germany gave up with Jews, without contemplating any distinctions between them. There was no more profound expression of the failure of multiculturalism than the Holocaust.

8. WESTERN INDIVIDUALISM

Nationalism offers commonality. Individualism refuses it.

Central to multiculturalism is a contradiction. Multiculturalists refuse commonality with their race while imagining commonality with other races, but those other races retain their commonalities: their nationalism. Multiculturalists are individualists.

On and about the first Saturday in February 2009, a hundred and seventy-three people died in bushfires sweeping rural Victoria. Among the escapees from the fires at Marysville was Peter Chambers. *"A situational definition had emerged,"* he wrote almost two weeks later, *"and it was a nationalist one: ugly Australian nationalism… refashioned into the comfortable and relaxed version innocuous enough for general consumption."*

He was the first person I'd heard perceive people supporting each other in face of the fires in terms of nationalism, but he was right. The fear of more than three hundred people dying came with a sense this wasn't just a crisis for the people involved but a national crisis. We'd responded with charity collections in shopping centres and from radios, televisions, and newspapers. Any sense of us feeling parts of a group, sharing victims' suffering, appalled Chambers. Good multiculturalists, citizens of the world, would've left them to roast.

"The fires were still burning," Chambers continued, *"but the smoke had cleared: there was a narrative (nationalist), there were the heroes (Aussie men), there were the victims (Aussie women and children), and there was the culprit (a swarthy arsonist with a funny surname, a hard drive full of kiddy p-rn, and a picture in the paper)."*

Chambers was horrified that people were hostile to a man who'd started a fire that killed twenty-one people. News reports described him merely as a Gippsland man thirty-nine years old interested in child pornography who'd been, ironically, a bushfire fighter. I'd not realised his surname was funny, nor seen his picture to know he was swarthy. In his hatred of racism, Chambers introduced race into something I'd not realised was racial.

Brendan Sokaluk was eventually convicted of ten counts of arson causing death. Then, I only saw him referred to as a Victorian man. He might've moved out of Gippsland.

Chambers went onto complain about a discussion of the fires on the television programme *Q & A*. Tania Major defended Australian values in what Chambers called a *"war footing,"* amidst her *"rant…stirring and incoherent."* Chambers mightn't have known Major was Aboriginal.

Even worse than a sense of national identity was a sense anything about it was good. Environmentalist Tim Flannery said Australia was special because "we have this ethic of mateship – we do care for each other in part because we do face such horrendous disasters as this." This was "just part of our character," but "we need to build on it, we need to make sure that we keep it alive, because more and more of us are becoming urbanised and detached from that view, but it's very precious, it really is precious. We've got to hold on to it."

At least Flannery had the excuse, suggested Chambers, of being caught up in the moment. Respite came from British-born surgeon Fiona Wood, who said "it's precious, this mateship in Australia, but it's not Australian, it's people. I believe in people. I believe in the power of people."

Yet, I overheard a Chinese woman at our children's preschool express her surprise at the generosity of Australians giving money for the bushfire victims, speaking as if no other people were so generous. She was right. The British-based Charities Aid Foundation would report Australia and New Zealand being the most generous donors of time and money to charity that year, at the head of a hundred and fifty-three countries accounting for ninety-five percent of the world's population. China was close to the bottom, barely higher than last-placed Madagascar. In 2012, America and Canada would head the list.

The end of Western racism and nationalism means all those reasons for feeling good about us become reasons to feel good about everyone else. They don't need to be good, if we are.

"There was no 'Australian spirit' in Marysville on Saturday afternoon," wrote Chambers. *"There were a lot of very frightened, scared, confused people doing whatever they had to do to try to save their houses and their lives. Something horrendous happened there, something that's difficult to comprehend, something that none of us, even the lucky ones, properly understand yet. I keep*

looking at the photos of me smiling in the town that morning, or relaxing in the house I stayed in that afternoon — a house that no longer exists, on the edge of a town that no longer exists. Then I turn to the media, hoping to find out exactly, to the minute, what the window was between escape and survival, existence and non-existence. And mostly all I can see is an orgy of nationalist self-love and self-pity. It's hard to know what's more alienating."

That was to say, the alienation white people feel from our country's love and pity is comparable to the alienation we'd feel from seeing our homes destroyed and being close to our deaths. Chambers would know.

Chambers went onto cite the words of a friend working at a college teaching English to immigrants in Melbourne. The college arranged a fundraising sausage sizzle for the bushfire appeal, culminating in a speech to the mostly Chinese students in which the school's director explained how lucky "they" were to be here and "see this." Chambers added the quotation marks to be clear *he* didn't distinguish the Chinese from us or Australia from the rest of the world. He was particularly distressed to hear the school's director tell them they'd learnt something about Australian spirit. "When we are in trouble," she told them, "we stick together."

Following her speech, there were cries of "Aussie, Aussie, Aussie, oi, oi, oi!"

Only one news report I saw mentioned the people in nearby Melbourne delighted at our deaths in those bushfires wreaking destruction. Like Sokaluk, their races and religions weren't mentioned. They were simply jihadists. Just in case we drew any inferences from them, Regional Islamic Council vice president Armeer Ali assured us they didn't represent the wider Muslim community. With those few words, we needn't worry.

When we think about Islam, we place great credence in what Muslim community leaders tell us Islam expects of Muslims. It matters more than what other Muslims think Islam expects of them, or what Muslims actually do.

American cities and towns accepted more than a hundred thousand Muslim Somali refugees from 1991 until 2015. Cedar Riverside, Minneapolis became known as Little Mogadishu.

In 2010, twenty-nine men and women involved with Somali gangs in Minneapolis and St Paul were indicted for a sex-trafficking ring that forced girls under eighteen years of age (some under fourteen years of age) into prostitution. The twenty-four count indictment unsealed in the District Court of the Middle District of Tennessee referred to three Minneapolis-based gangs (the Somali Outlaws, Somali Mafia, and Lady Outlaws) transporting girls between St Paul, Nashville, and Columbus (cities with large Somali populations) and committing burglaries, car theft, and credit card fraud. Their religion wasn't reported, although Omar Jamal, a Somali advocate in Minnesota, claimed Islam forbids those crimes.

"The American identity is dead," said one of six Minnesota men who'd repeatedly sought to join Islamic State forces in Syria, in a recorded conversation before their arrest in April 2015. "Even if I get caught, whatever, I'm through with America. Burn my I.D."

"To be clear, we have a terror recruitment problem in Minnesota," admitted American attorney Andrew Luger at a press conference in Minneapolis afterwards, referring to the Somali refugees there and in St Paul. There was "no master recruiter, radicalising your son, your brother, your neighbour," but a mass of recruitment. "It could be their best friend right here in town."

In 2011, Prime Minister David Cameron said multiculturalism had failed and contributed to the threat of terrorism in the United Kingdom. He didn't propose any alternative, question immigration, or obviously change any policies because of his realisation. Instead, he said the European Union should admit Muslim Turkey.

After former Victorian premier Jeff Kennett said in 2011 that migrants to Australia should accept the Australian way of life, anthropology graduate and journalist Tory Shepherd called phrases such as *"way of life"* empty and dangerous. *"'We' don't have a way of life,"* she wrote, finding no common thread between the outback and rural Tasmania, between the Adelaide suburbs and miners flying in and out of Perth. *"We don't even share all the same values – just look at what happens when you talk about religion, abortion, euthanasia, politics, social welfare…and multiculturalism. There is no unified 'we'."*

Yet, we'll talk of other races having ways of life, especially indigenous peoples we shouldn't have disturbed. Hers was a statement of the West's loss of nations and races, made not with an observer's disinterest but gleefully to make her point. Western races were unified when we enjoyed nationalism and racism, when values meant less than they've come to mean.

While we can't find common threads with our compatriots, we're supposed to feel them with the rest of the world. *"Altogether now!"* beamed the caption to Tom Lee's photograph accompanying

Shepherd's article, with a smiling myriad of different races wearing different clothes. *"We are the world…"*

"Failed social policies, poverty and alienation, and a complex blend of cultural factors have led to problems in the UK," wrote Shepherd. Whatever *"a complex blend of cultural factors"* meant, it presumably wasn't multiculturalism. By *"problems,"* she presumably referred to events like the bombings of the London Underground the first Thursday of July 2005, which killed fifty-two people (as well as the Muslim suicide bombers) and injured more than seven hundred.

"Some Muslims hold truly abhorrent beliefs," she explained. *"Most Muslims do not, in the same way that most Christians do not believe homosexuals should be stoned."*

I've never heard any Christians saying homosexuals should be stoned, although news services would enthusiastically report any who did. Three years later, they reported Oklahoma election candidate Scott Esk citing Biblical condemnation of homosexuality. Esk needed to explain he wasn't calling for homosexuals to be stoned. The Bible sees Christ's death as atonement for sins.

"All religious extremists are problematic," wrote Shepherd, equating terrorism not with one religion but all religions. *"Australia needs to be wary of extremism, not multiculturalism."*

Blaming terrorism on America and her alliances, Shepherd suggested monoculturalism created a bigger risk of terrorism than multiculturalism. *"Imagine if a country set itself up as both a close ally of the US and a country that did not accept anyone from a different culture. You'd have a prime target then."* I'm still waiting news of Islamic terrorism in America's staunch allies: homogenous Japan and homogenous South Korea.

Shepherd had a solution that didn't discriminate between religions. *"And history has shown that terrorists are not necessarily born – they are bred."* (I've not seen such a history, unless she meant blaming Muslim terrorism upon our supposed maltreatment of them.) *"So you'd have to ban… well, maybe religion altogether."*

Apparently, banning religion isn't extremism. It must be multiculturalism. The more menacing Muslims become, the more we wish we could end all religion. We start with our own.

We don't defend our countries from Islam, because we don't countenance the collective identities upon which such a defence would be predicated. We don't group Muslim terrorists or their victims.

At least seven Muslims murdered a hundred and thirty people and injured three hundred and sixty-eight others, many seriously, in a series of co-ordinated attacks on a concert, restaurant, football stadium, and other popular venues in Paris the second Friday of November 2015. President François Hollande called them attacks on humanity, but they weren't. They were attacks upon France. Until we acknowledge we're the targets in this conflict, we'll never escape it.

Among the terrorists' bodies was a Syrian refugee's passport. "Australia needs to have better scrutiny vetting refugees," responded Australian senator Jacqui Lambie.

"*Her's is the language of Nazism*," complained our parish Anglican church treasurer James on the Facebook website, the third Thursday in November 2015. Any hint of Western borders or interest in protecting our compatriots from suffering and death had become Nazism.

We've not simply lost the sense our forebears fought and died for peace. We've rejected the idea. "*There is no way to peace*," declares a tile below the Peace Bell in Cowra. "*Peace is the way.*"

The ten Rainbow Family members espoused "peace, love, and harmony" at their School of Happiness commune in the northern New South Wales town of Tenterfield. The middle Sunday of April 2012, Ryan Pringle came to the community, but he quickly became aggressive, took the members hostage, assaulted them, and threatened them with a crossbow and knife. Their nine-hour ordeal ended when police shot him dead.

Rainbow Family members defended police, saying they had little choice. We understand the need sometimes to defend ourselves from white people better than we see a need to defend ourselves from other races.

"*Igitur qui desiderat pacem, praeparet bellum*," wrote the Roman military strategist Vegetius around about the year 400. I first heard it expressed "*Si vis pacem, para bellum*," sixteen hundred years later, watching the most violent film I'd seen, *The Punisher*. "If you want peace, prepare for war."

The necessity to defend peace remains, but ours isn't the peace our forebears craved. The peace we crave isn't for millennia. It's for the moment.

Ours isn't peace for nations but an individualist pacifism. We've become lone individuals, for fear relationships might draw us to battle. We don't fight, kill, or die for anyone else. We don't do anything for anyone else.

Whatever the West is, we're not defending it. That's more than our right, as individuals. It's our expectation.

Rather than the freedom that country can be, freedom is ours alone, tucked in our tiny homes in our shrinking neighbourhoods. We've become careful about where we walk by night and day, without questioning it. We lock our doors and hide. It's our peace of mind, in the hollows of our heads. Our pacifism is so terrified of war, we dare not step outside, but proudly demand our compatriots not fight on our behalf. Ours is the peace America's President John Kennedy rejected in his State of the Union address the second Monday of January 1963. "The mere absence of war is not peace."

We'd rather be dead than be wrong. Faced with a choice between fighting for life and lying down to die, ours is a soulless surrender to fate.

When a survey reported that something like a third of Sydneysiders had left a railway carriage or train because a person they feared was Muslim had entered, we had immediate disdain for those bigots. I imagined us watching with contempt a white woman move from her seat because of the swarthy-faced man wearing a backpack who'd sat down beside her. We might even venture forth a self-satisfied smile that we'd stayed behind, before his backpack blasts us both to our free-willing deaths.

9. THE PEACE OF NATIONS

In 1986, as it so often does, the threat of war hung over Europe. "*Whoever hates war will never find peace*," declared graffiti on white hoarding around a construction site near the Sydney Opera House, "*whoever loves peace will always find it.*"

Our forebears across Europe, the Americas, and Australasia loved peace. In pursuit of peace, necessity sometimes demanded they fight, kill, and die. We now equate justice, freedom, and security with abandoning our nations and race. They equated them with defending theirs.

Other races suffering wars and massacres haven't made the same presumptions and pledges we now have; history makes them treasure their nations more. Race and nation remain matters of life and death: their own.

Jewish nationalism saves Jews from another Holocaust. Israel wins wars knowing that a hundred million Arabs can afford to lose a thousand wars and survive, but Jews can't afford to lose any. Its survival since 1948 is testament to not just Jewish resourcefulness, but nationalism.

Western nationalism disgusts us. Other people's nationalism doesn't.

Egypt's President Anwar Sadat was a nationalist and Muslim. Israel's Prime Minister Menachem Begin was no less a nationalist. In the 1978 Camp David Accords, the two men boldly affirmed each other's countries, bravely defending their own. Peace cost Israel a fortune in money and land. It cost Sadat the respect of fellow Muslim Arabs and ultimately his life, but he grew Egypt as few Egyptians had. Both men saved people's lives.

In an old television interview broadcast after his assassination in 1981, Sadat said he abandoned communism after looking out an East European hotel window. I think it was early one morning and he saw a woman as old as his mother who should've been resting. Instead, she was sweeping the street.

Demanding work of the people, communism offered no grace

or compassion, but what he saw in that woman wasn't communism. It was Europe without nation: without compassionate nationalism or nationalist compassion.

A decade after we finished our Business studies, my Chinese friend James Lee was a guest in my home. In a conversation about Middle Eastern conflict, he believed Israel could solve its security problems with Palestinian Arabs by building an impenetrable wall, much longer and larger than anything already built, but hadn't because the borders it wanted weren't those in place.

There can be no peace without security, and no security without borders. A people are only free when they keep at bay those who'd deny them their freedom.

"*I made a promise that if I am not able to achieve success because of some Caucasians, I will kill as many of them as possible,*" American-born African Hasan Akbar, formerly Mark Fidel Kools, wrote in his diary in 1992. "*A Muslim should see himself as a Muslim only,*" he wrote in 1993. "*His loyalty should be to Islam only.*" In 1998, he joined the American Army. "*I may not have killed any Muslims,*" he wrote after America invaded Iraq in 2003, "*but being in the Army is the same thing. I may have to make a choice very soon on who to kill.*" He chose to kill two American soldiers.

We dare not wonder whether Western countries can fight wars in Muslim countries with Muslims among our soldiers; we don't want wars anyway. Multiracial militaries are supposed to be less able to make war, but ours compromise our capacity for defence.

On the fifth of November (Guy Fawkes Night) 2009 at the Fort Hood military base in Texas, Major Nidal Malik Hasan, an American-born Arab, murdered thirteen American soldiers. "The important thing is for everyone not to jump to conclusions," said retired general Wesley Clark that night on the *Cable News Network*. A string of political, military, and media figures expressed the same sentiments.

Three days later, General George Casey was still telling the same network: "We can't jump to conclusions."

That was in spite of Hasan proselytizing Islam within the ranks, speaking out against wars the American Army was fighting in Muslim countries, and wanting not to fight in Afghanistan. He'd visited websites associated with Islamist violence and wrote justifications for Muslim suicide bombings. Shortly before the shootings, he told a neighbour he was going "to do good work for god." As he gunned down his fellow soldiers, he shouted *"Allahu Akbar!"*

He'd even carried a business card for his work away from the army base, calling himself a psychiatrist and *"SoA,"* meaning Soldier of Allah. This war comes with business cards, but we don't pay attention.

Hasan's military superiors at the Walter Reed National Military Medical Centre hadn't just noticed his interest in Muslim nationalism. They'd commended him for it. *"He has a keen interest in Islamic culture and faith and has shown capacity to contribute to our psychological understanding of Islamic nationalism and how it may relate to events of national security and Army interest in the Middle East and Asia,"* supervisors wrote in an evaluation report the first day of July 2009. *"Maj. Hasan has great potential as an Army officer."*

Hasan was earning a master's degree in public health through a two-year fellowship in disaster and preventive psychiatry. A military report completed the second Friday of March 2009 said he had *"outstanding moral integrity."*

Army prosecutors at his court martial accused Hasan of waging jihad with the thirteen murders. He didn't challenge the accusation.

There'd been thirty-three Muslim plots against the American military in the decade since 2001. Rather than trying to prevent more attacks, the Pentagon's eighty-six page report into the Fort Hood massacre was a wondrous achievement in ensuring there should be no link with Islam. It never mentioned Hasan by name, less that connote anything.

"The report demonstrates that we are unwilling to identify and confront the real enemy of political Islam," responded a former military colleague of Hasan, speaking privately because he'd been ordered not to talk about the case. "Political correctness has brainwashed us to the point that we no longer understand our heritage and cannot admit who, or what, the enemy stands for."

A Department of Defence letter called the massacre *"workplace violence."* Murdering thirteen soldiers with cries of *"Allahu Akbar!"* wasn't about Islam, but about occupational health and safety. (I couldn't help but look uneasily around the offices in which I sat.)

Early in 2013, the *News Limited Network* chronicled recent mass killings in America. It described Hasan only as an army psychiatrist.

On the middle Friday of July 2015, the *Australian Broadcasting Corporation News* website headed stories about a drunken tennis player in Miami, snowfalls in New South Wales, newly released images of a Malaysian aircraft downed a year earlier, and a hostage siege in Western Australia. It then reported Muslims gathering for feasts around Australia to mark the end of Ramadan, with photographs and detail about its religious significance.

Only then it reported a gunman killing four American marines at a Navy and Marine Corps Reserve Centre and wounding others at a recruitment centre in Tennessee, without mention of Islam or Muslims. The killer was a Kuwaiti-born American citizen Mohammod Youssuf Abdulazeez, who'd graduated from the University of Chattanooga in 2012 with a bachelor's degree in electrical engineering. "He was friendly, funny, kind," said Kagan Wagner, who'd attended Red Bank High School with him. "They were your average Chattanooga family."

Average Chattanooga families didn't murder marines. Insisting people not jump to conclusions, Department of Homeland Security secretary Jeh Johnson warned "there are many unconfirmed and possibly false reports about events."

By that, he might've referred to Abdulazeez's words on his website the previous Monday. Muslims should not let "*the opportunity to submit to Allah... pass you by.*"

Still, journalists refused to speculate on his motive. The killer "was a nice kid from a nice family, and he was as American as anybody else," insisted one *Cable News Network* reporter. Officials called the attack domestic, not Islamic, terror. A fifth marine died later.

In our spirit of inclusion, the Pentagon invited a Muslim cleric to a service for Petty Officer First Class Michael Strange and other Navy SEALs killed in Afghanistan in August 2011. Speaking in Arabic his audience couldn't understand, the cleric damned the dead infidels.

This was all in an army that instructed its young officers to read Sun Tzu's *The Art of War*. The book commanded warriors to know their enemy.

A place in which people kill freely isn't a country. Our forebears risked their lives in wars but could come home to peace. Our soldiers no longer can. Without nations, we're intrinsically insecure.

Michael Oluwatobi Adebowale and Michael Adebolaj were born in Britain into devout Christian Nigerian families and well educated, but Christianity isn't the Nigerian religion. In May 2013, they saw Lee Rigby, a drummer with the Royal Regiment of Fusiliers who'd fought in Afghanistan, walking along John Wilson Street two hundred yards from the Royal Artillery Barracks in Woolwich, London. They ran down the devoted, young father of a two-year-old son with a car, before hacking him to death with a meat cleaver and a butcher's knife, shouting *"Allahu Akbar!"*

They wanted passers-by to film them trying to behead him. "By Allah," one told the cameras, "we swear by almighty Allah, we will never stop fighting until you leave us alone."

Multiculturalism makes that impossible. We can't leave other races and religions alone when we share the same countries, cities, and streets. La Trobe University sociologist Ramon Spaaij said the killer's words to the cameras were declarations that "no one is safe, anyone walking his dog could be butchered."

"It's a scene that might have come out of Rwanda or the Congo," wrote journalists Deborah Snow and Nick Miller. *"Yet the setting is…south-east London, with the surreal touch of a red double-decker bus in the background."*

Multiculturalism was supposed to make our countries blueprints for a brave new world without war, but we've simply brought wars to our streets. Removing our borders created more conflict.

Immediately after the murder of Rigby, military authorities warned British troops not to wear their uniforms outside bases, before the British government's Cobra Crisis Committee decided the next morning not to respond with such a message. Prime Minister David Cameron blasted the attack not as a betrayal of Britain but as "a betrayal of Islam and of the Muslim communities who give so much to this country," without specifying what they gave. He then flew to Ibiza on holiday.

British Broadcasting Corporation political editor Nick Robinson apologised for having quoted police sources who described the attackers as being of Muslim appearance. *"That phrase 'of Muslim appearance' clearly offended some who demanded to know what it could possibly mean,"* he wrote the next day. *"Others were concerned that it was a racist generalisation."* We spoke only of the Woolwich attack.

"He was really friendly and really polite and there was never anything to suggest he would be caught up in anything like this," said British hairdresser Justine Rigden, who'd been romantically involved with Adebolaj for a year when they were teenagers. "He was just this normal, regular boy."

Three days after Rigby's slaying, Private First Class Cedric Cordier was one of three French soldiers patrolling the busy underground corridors beneath the *Arche de la Défense* in the Parisian business, shopping, and transport district. Shortly before six o'clock that Saturday evening, he was approached from behind and stabbed in the neck with a knife or cutter that narrowly missed his carotid artery. The assailant was North African, who'd been filmed praying before the attack.

The third Monday in October 2014, Martin Couture-Rouleau, who'd converted to Islam, drove his car into two Canadian soldiers in Quebec, killing one. The following day, Michael Zehaf-Bibeau shot dead young Corporal Nathan Cirillo on ceremonial sentry duty at the Canadian National War Memorial in Ottawa.

Sometimes, there are hints of change. Several years earlier, when I came to collect my eldest daughter (a friend of his daughter) from his home, a senior counsel friend of mine gently rebuked my second son for being wary of a man appearing Muslim we'd seen in the street. Two evenings after Rigby's death, Alister and I were among the participants in a conversation in our local parliamentarian's offices. He wondered whether many more Muslims supported, or at least sympathised with, Muslim terrorism than we thought.

He also spoke of people congregating naturally by race, including the Chinese among his examples. A young Chinese man with us concurred.

White people concerned about the changing places in which we live don't want to don jackboots and goose-step through Nuremberg, any more than Japanese maintaining their racial and national integrity are about to invade Manchuria. Japan has enjoyed more peace than we've known since 1945.

If the West wanted peace between peoples, we'd want races safe with their religions within nations, but we don't want peace. We want multiculturalism.

For us to find security again, we'd have to love peace more than we hate war. We'd feel part of a people with race and religion; everyone else does. We'd believe in countries, distinct from each other, allowing them not just for others but also for us. Peace requires peoples determining their destinies behind borders. Like neighbours, we need fences not to fight.

10. MUSLIM NATIONALISM

Colonel Muammar Gaddafi's Libya was among several regimes in the world to sponsor terrorism against the West. The first Saturday of April 1986, a bomb at the La Belle disco in West Berlin killed two American servicemen and a Turkish woman. America retaliated, for which Muslims were furious.

The only man convicted of the bombing of Pan Am flight 103 four days before Christmas 1988 was former Libyan agent Abdel Basset al-Megrahi, a father of five. In 2001, a Scottish court sentenced him to life in prison, but a little thing like killing two hundred and seventy people, including eleven Scots on the ground in the town of Lockerbie, wasn't going to keep us from compassion. While still British prime minister, Tony Blair began a process leading to the Scottish government releasing al-Megrahi in 2009, supposedly because he was terminally ill and would die in three months.

Britain wanted Libyan oil contracts. Never was the West less interested in the deaths of our own.

On al-Megrahi's return to Tripoli, hundreds of young Libyans gathered at the airport to welcome him home. In a country where large public gatherings were rare and usually tightly controlled, they cheered and waved Libyan flags. His car sped away to his large villa, where a huge tent accommodated friends and family congratulating him on his release, including his eldest son studying at university. His family asked journalists not to film or record any comments, although amidst the partying were cheers of *"Allahu Akbar!"*

Those festivities didn't diminish our views about Libyans, Arabs, or Muslims. "I don't think the reception for Mister al-Megrahi was appropriate in Libya," said Alex Salmond, first minister of Scotland, as a well-reserved schoolmistress might speak of a child whispering while another child was addressing her class. "I don't think that was wise, and I don't think that was the right thing to do." Al-Megrahi would live another three years, without regretting the Lockerbie bombing.

Western lawyers champion the rights of Muslims. So do Muslim lawyers.

The 2010 Muslim Advocates conference in San Francisco applauded American attorney general Eric Holder after he assured them he would protect Muslim's civil liberties. "We have very serious concerns about F.B.I. surveillance tactics that are used," said executive director Farhana Khera, referring to the Federal Bureau of Investigations. "We believe that law enforcement has an important job to protect us as a country, but they should do so mindful of the rules of justice and fairness that are at the core of our criminal justice system."

Muslim lawyers are more demonstrative in Muslim countries. In his sermon the first Friday of December 2010, Imam Maulana Yousuf Qureshi offered six thousand dollars to anyone who murdered Asia Bibi, a Christian woman accused of blaspheming Allah. When Punjab governor Salman Taseer defended Bibi, Mumtaz Qadri murdered the governor.

Pakistani lawyers didn't rush to defend the Christian alleged blasphemer. They rushed to defend the Muslim assassin. Four hundred of them offered Qadri free legal services. When Qadri was being led to court the first Thursday of January 2011, lawyers showered him with rose petals.

When émigrés to the West offend Islam, we cop culpability too. While imprisoned in an American gaol, a Christian Egyptian named Nakoula Basseley Nakoula prepared the script for a film ridiculing Mohammed. A thirteen-minute trailer popularly known as *Innocence of Muslims* was produced in California and published on the YouTube website in 2012.

Muslims around the world protested. On Tuesday, the eleventh day of September, Egyptians climbed the walls of the American embassy in Cairo, tore apart an American flag, and replaced it with a black al-Qaeda flag.

In Sydney on Saturday, up to five hundred Muslims including children carrying banners such as *"Behead all those who insult the prophet"* and *"Our dead are in paradise, your dead are in hell"* stormed towards the American consulate. Speakers denounced America and critics of Islam, denigrating the immorality of Christians. Six policemen were injured, two hospitalised. Two vehicles were damaged. A protester taken away by ambulance managed to spit at officers and chant "*Allahu Akbar!*"

Abdullah Sary insisted the protesters came in peace. "The anger comes from the fact if you attack the Prophet, you are attacking our way of life," he explained. "This was a non-violent protest, but people don't like seeing their brothers attacked by dogs and ending up in hospital."

Westerners no longer claim to have ways of life. We don't defend our brothers.

As if it were all no more than a different way of walking, Premier Barry O'Farrell told *Sky News* the next day that Muslim leaders with whom he'd discussed the protests considered them out of step. "What we shouldn't do is condemn the great bulk of Muslims by the actions of a few extremists," he said, "any more than you should do with Catholics, Buddhists, Hindus, or others." We never cease distinguishing wrongdoers from the rest, or equating religions. "Episodes like yesterday really do attack what is one of the great foundations of our success, which is our multiculturalism."

"I do not believe that the people on the streets of Sydney yesterday were truly representative of Islam," agreed federal Liberal Party leader Tony Abbott. "I don't believe that the ugliness we saw on the streets of Sydney fairly reflects the Islamic people of our country." He had no need to justify his view.

Melbourne comedienne Catherine Deveny, who attacked Christianity in her stage show 'God Is Bullshit,' didn't defend the film-maker. She defended the protesters. "*Protests,*" she wrote the next day on the Twitter website, "*are a healthy byproduct of free speech and democracy.*"

The *Sydney Morning Herald* newspaper characterised Muslims as victims. 'Police gas Sydney protesters,' was its headline.

We didn't condemn Muslims for the protests. We condemned Christians for the film.

Journalist Paul McGeough blamed "*crackpot Christian fundamentalists in California*" for "*the grossly offensive mockery of the prophet Muhammad – rightly described by Hillary Clinton as 'disgusting and reprehensible' – being revealed as the deliberately provocative work of exiled Egyptian Christian Copts in the US and their deranged fellow travellers from the American Christian right.*" He wrote of "*the Christian crazies in California.*"

Nobody defended the majority of Christians who don't make

films. Nor were we so racist as to distinguish Egyptian from American Christians.

McGeough provided a spirited defence of Muslims. *"But when for decades whole populations have been treated as an inconsequential mob, some of them can hardly be blamed for behaving as such when provoked. Their social landscapes have been cruel, intellectually barren spaces, in which broken-down education and state censorship fostered ignorance and narrowness."* What sounded like Western governments were, apparently, past governments in Muslim countries.

"The naivety of some as they grappled for understanding was touching," continued McGeough. *"There was genuine puzzlement on the part of one imam who spoke to The New York Times in Kandahar, Afghanistan. 'I ask the government of America,' he said, 'why did they allow a person to insult a man, Muhammad, when by insulting him they sadden the whole Muslim world, and create hatred towards Americans?'"*

We don't imagine there being a Christian world, not anymore. America's onus is to censor anything offensive to Muslims.

"I am the prime minister of a nation, of which most are Muslims, that has declared anti-Semitism a crime against humanity," said Turkey's Prime Minister Recep Tayyip Erdoğan that week, "but the West hasn't recognised Islamophobia as a crime against humanity. It has encouraged it."

Pakistan's parliament demanded that country's leaders call on the United Nations to take action against the film-makers. Indonesia's President Susilo Bambang Yudhoyono called on the Organisation of Islamic Co-operation (which had long pressed for a United Nations resolution condemning what it considered the defamation of religion) and United Nations "to mull over international protocol to prevent such things like this from happening again."

Emad Abdel Ghaffour, leader of Egypt's Salafist Nour Party, called upon the United Nations to criminalise the contempt of Islam and Mohammed. "The voice of reason in the West will prevail if there is mutual respect, dialogue, and efficient lobbying for this critical resolution," he told *Reuters* news service. "A proposal to look into the root causes of the obvious racism against Muslims and Arabs as the recent fierce campaign against their Islamic beliefs shows is much needed."

Australian foreign minister Bob Carr was concerned about the Sydney protests upsetting people, but only Muslims. "It's a more nuanced story," he said on Monday, "and we've got to think about the hurt and the pain of Australian Muslims, loyal Australians, when they saw that stupid and dangerous and repugnant lunatic fringe – a hundred of them, a mere hundred of them – on Saturday night's T.V."

His was the lowest estimate of the number of protesters I read. He also presumed Muslims were loyal Australians when Australians were no longer loyal.

"It concerns me deeply," said Carr, "and I understand the response of Australians – those of Islamic heritage, those of other backgrounds – who look at the sights and hear the sounds of that demonstration and think: 'Why do you linger in Australia? There would be other countries where you'd be happier, where you'd be more fulfilled.'"

Violent protests don't make people question multiculturalism. They make people more confident in it.

"Far from being an assault on multiculturalism," Jewish businessman Frank Lowy told the Multicultural Council in Canberra on Wednesday evening, "last weekend can be a sign of the strength and maturity of our multicultural society." It was a strange sense of strength and maturity.

As always, we focused upon the Muslim leaders' public statements. *"The Islamic summit alone was a triumphant assertion of multiculturalism,"* declared journalist Mike Carlton the following Saturday, *"an affirmation by the Muslim community that it respects Australian law and wishes to live here in peace and harmony."* He dismissed the protesters as *"a bus load of deluded yobs,"* while directing his vitriol at the *"nutters on the fringes,"* by which he meant Australians criticising Muslims. *"We are the most successful multicultural society the world has known,"* he insisted without explanation, unless he meant his two older children liking multiculturalism so much after his grandmother was such a racist.

Perhaps Australian multiculturalism is the most successful the world has known because nobody died in the Sydney protest. Fifty or more died in Muslim protests in other countries.

"Criminologists nail it again," wrote my lawyer friend Anthony with approval on his Facebook computer page, defining Mohamad Tabbaa not by his race or religion but his job, as white people do. Tabbaa, from the University of Melbourne, researched issues around discrimination against Muslims. (Universities don't research

discrimination *by* Muslims.)

Tabbaa blamed the Muslim protest in Sydney on Western military action in Muslim countries and the treatment of Muslims in Burma, China, Kashmir, Palestine, Chechnya, *"and the many other places around the world where they witness injustice and persecution."* (They gave us no credit that a day or two before the protest, Australia announced accepting a thousand refugees from the bloody Syrian civil war, where Muslims were killing Muslims.) *"So no, this is not entirely about some poor-quality YouTube clip."*

"To begin with, many Muslims in Australia do not simply give up their identity as belonging to a global community merely because they happen to live in Australia. Many have not bought the liberal idea of individualism, and so see events happening on the other side of the planet as personally related to them. So, when a Muslim woman is killed collecting firewood in Afghanistan, these youth are angered at the fact that their sister was murdered. When a Muslim man is crushed to death in Palestine, they lament the loss of their brother. It may not make sense to a Western audience, but that doesn't matter. This is what is angering our youth, and until we start discussing it honestly and genuinely, the confusion will remain."

Were we to list instances of Christians or Westerners being attacked by Muslims, we'd be called Islamophobic, but we *have* bought into the Western idea of individualism. There is no Muslim individualism.

Tabbaa condemned the Muslim community leaders saying those words we like to hear, which we insist are the norm among Muslims. *"Rather than voicing their grievances, they see their leaders capitulating to representatives of the governments they accuse of Muslim oppression. Instead of protecting them from what are seen as some of the harshest anti-terrorism laws in the world, they see their leaders thanking police for raiding Muslim homes; they see their leaders as siding against them, rather than with them; they feel betrayed."*

We could say the same of Western leaders. Protecting people is nationalism.

Muslims aren't just defending each other. They're advancing each other.

Australian-born father of four Khaled Sharrouf finished his four years in prison for plotting a terrorist attack in Sydney. In 2013, several years later, he flew out of Australia on his brother's passport to fight with the burgeoning Islamic State of Iraq and the Levant. Only after posing for a photograph in military fatigues with a military vehicle in Iraq did the Australian government cancel his disability pension of seven hundred and sixty-six dollars a fortnight.

The only meaningful collective identities are race and religion. Biology and deity matter.

Religious nationalism is predicated not upon personal belief, but collective identity. So little did Yusuf Sarwar and Mohammed Ahmed know of their faith before setting off from Birmingham to fight in Syria in 2014, they bought the books *Islam for Dummies* and *The Koran for Dummies*. Ignorance of the detail doesn't mean people lack conviction.

Quoting Muslim academics claiming the Koran teaches peace and tolerance, journalist Emma Reynolds seemed to lecture Islamic State to surrender their weaponry, but she was really lecturing the West to ignore Muslim terror and intolerance. Storm clouds don't turn back because the forecast weather was sunshine.

We respect Muslim nationalism identifying with fellow Muslims as victims. We refuse to identify them with fellow Muslims doing wrong.

"Muslims have suffered the most at the hands of extremism," claimed America's President Barack Obama, in a speech telling the United Nations General Assembly those thirteen minutes of film mocking Mohammed offended Americans as well as Muslims because Americans welcomed all races and religions. "The future must not belong to those who slander the prophet of Islam."

11. SOLIDARITY

Two generations after the Second World War, our young men still set off to war. Now, they fight against us.

In their first year of high school, my eldest son's Persian friend David told him that Christians were terrorists, citing David Hicks. Through Persian eyes, the South Australian captured late in 2001 at an al-Qaeda training camp in Afghanistan was born and would always be Christian because he was Western. We agreed, referring to him as Hicks because it made him like us instead of the name he'd adopted in 1999: Muhammed Dawood. Bad white people remain Christian, even if they think they're not.

Other races haven't bought into Western individualism. Neither really have we, as Hicks brought into sharp relief. Australians who had rejected loyalty to our compatriots for being nationalistic found patriotic fervour to defend Hicks, or any other Westerner accused of terrorism against us.

Hicks reportedly renounced Islam after being imprisoned for his terrorist affiliations. It was a shame he hadn't beforehand, but people do all sorts of strange things in gaol.

In 2011, Hicks said he'd converted to Islam for a sense of belonging. Given his parents had separated when he was ten years old, that need for belonging would've been particularly acute.

White people embrace the Muslim crescent and sword for its nationalism and self-belief the West has forsaken: a crusade since the failings of communism became inescapable. Western revolutionaries fighting their countries, race, and selves care no more what the Koran says about anything than twentieth-century communists cared what *Das Kapital* had to say.

We respond to Muslim terrorism not by echoing its loyalties, but by further rejecting ours. English girl Samantha Lewthwaite was eleven years old when her parents divorced, devastating her. She found comfort in the strong family ethic of Muslims; the togetherness of nationalism is the togetherness of family. The widow of a 2005 London suicide bomber, she claimed to be another victim of terrorism, before becoming known as the White Widow at war with the West.

Maybe the real problems are family and friends, which Western individualism discount. Monash University researcher Shandon Harris-Hogan found family connections and friendships linked fifty-seven people into terrorist networks in Australia through the twelve years to 2012. Similar studies of Fatah, Hamas, Hezbollah, Palestinian Islamic Jihad, and Turkish terrorists revealed about one in five were recruited by relatives. Seven in ten terrorists had been close friends with other terrorists in their youths.

We maintain our individualism when white people suffer, refusing to side with our race or religion. When people of other races and religions suffer, we step in.

Nobody minded seven-year-old white boy Josh Welch being removed from a Maryland school for chewing a pop-tart into the shape of a pistol and pretending to shoot other students with it. Nor did we care when sixteen-year-old white boy Alex Stone had his locker searched and was arrested, handcuffed, charged with disorderly conduct, and suspended from a South Carolina school for three days because he wrote a short story in which he imagined shooting a dinosaur.

Fourteen-year-old Muslim boy Ahmed Mohamed brought to a Texas school in 2015 a beeping, strange-looking homemade device, which school officials thought was a bomb. He too was removed from class, handcuffed, and suspended from school.

It turned out to be a clock, but the precautions we take against white children are unacceptable prejudices against other children. President Barack Obama invited Mohamed to the White House, Methodist former secretary of state Hilary Clinton sent him a message of support, Jewish entrepreneur Mark Zuckerberg invited him into the Facebook offices, and Roman Catholic entrepreneur Jack Dorsey's Twitter company invited him to be an intern.

In August 2013, Swedish women including lawmakers Asa Romson and Veronica Palm expressed their solidarity with a pregnant Muslim woman assaulted while wearing a hijab in Stockholm by publishing photographs of themselves wearing headscarves. In an article in the *Aftonbladet* newspaper, campaigners wrote that they wanted to draw attention to the "*discrimination that affects Muslim women*" in Sweden and to "*ensure that Swedish Muslim women are guaranteed the right to... religious freedom.*" They called upon *"the prime minister and other politicians to take action to stop the march of fascism."*

We'd reached a time when fascism means any Western resistance to Islam: the West's last stand. We refuse to fight other races or religions. We keep waging World War II against our own.

In Britain, a representative of the One Law for All campaign 'Siding with the Oppressor: The Pro-Islamist Left' telephoned the offices of the Unite Against Fascism organisation in 2013 to ask its views about Islamic fascism. The reply was there was "no such thing."

Calling Islam fascist makes it political rather than religious, lumping it with European fascism, but Islamic fascism is another Western construct separating Muslim terror from Islam. There is only Islam, in all its forms.

Among the vice chairmen of Unite against Fascism was Azad Ali. He'd said of democracy that "if it means, you know, at the expense of not implementing the sharia, no one's gonna agree with that."

Ali was also affairs co-ordinator for the Islamic Forum of Europe, which came out of Jamaat-e-Islami. Jamaat-e-Islami said Islam obliged Muslims to kill British and American soldiers. Locked in our endless fighting of fascism, our allies are all other races and religions, whatever their beliefs.

Jesus Christ was one of several religious figures satirised in pictures drawn by twelve Danish cartoonists and published in the Danish newspaper *Jyllands-Posten* in 2005. The West's rejection of religion had stopped making blasphemy a crime or even offensive, provided it related to Christianity.

Unfortunately, the cartoonists also satirised Mohammed. Muslims around the world leapt into protests in which more than a hundred people died, furious that the cartoons insinuated Islam was a violent religion.

Jytte Klausen's book *The Cartoons That Shook the World* described the Muslim fury. It dared not reproduce the cartoons.

A French supermarket in the Carrefour chain responded with solidarity, but not with fellow Europeans. That would be racist. Besides, it had three Danish customers against innumerable Muslim ones. *"Dear Clients,"* it greeted customers in a notice posted in Arabic, *"We express solidarity with the Islamic and Egyptian community. Carrefour doesn't carry Danish products."* Ours is selective solidarity, no less than nationalism.

"It is a known fact," remarked a Danish court rejecting a lawsuit by Muslim groups against *Jyllands-Posten*, "that acts of terror have been carried out in the name of Islam and it is not illegal to make satire out of this relationship." Depicting Muslims as terrorists would have been illegal. The Organisation of the Islamic Conference, a league of fifty-seven Muslim nations, complained the decision could provoke Islamophobia. It had learnt the words of the West well.

In the Oslo District Court in 2012, Judge Oddmund Svarteberg sentenced a Uighur with Norwegian citizenship, Mikael Davud, and an Iraqi Kurd living in Norway, Shawan Sadek Saeed Bujak, to gaol for plotting to attack *Jyllands-Posten* and murder one of the cartoonists, Kurt Westergaard. They "planned the attack together with al-Qaeda." (Norway's anti-terror laws didn't apply to individuals, so their guilt depended upon conspiracy.) Investigators believed they were the same al-Qaeda operatives behind attacks planned against the New York subway system and a British shopping mall in 2009.

Alisher Abdullaev, an Uzbek who'd changed his name to David Jakobsen and became a Norwegian citizen, was convicted of helping them acquire explosives, although he later assisted police in their investigation. (He must have been one of those good Muslims.)

Instead of embracing the nationalism that other races retain, we embrace other races. We think they need common defence from us, as Jews did through the Holocaust.

The second Wednesday night of April 2009, Dutch public television station Nederland 2 broadcast the programme *Devil's Advocate*. In spite of many years of al-Qaeda boasting of its success with the 2001 terrorist attacks on America, attorney Gerard Spong convinced a Dutch jury that it had all been a product of Western propaganda: that al-Qaeda head Osama bin Mohammed bin Awad bin Laden (born in 1957 in Jeddah, Saudi Arabia) wasn't responsible, although he was a terrorist who'd "misused Islam." It was a little like saying Adolf Hitler was innocent of the Holocaust, although he was a despot who'd misused Nazism.

Spong was no less passionate about exploiting Dutch law and justice away from television cameras. He'd represented Red Army terrorists seeking refugee status in the Netherlands from West

Germany and defended alleged child murderers and drug dealers. Spong had every reason to champion all the rights he could find, being a Guyana-born bisexual Sephardic Jew with a penchant for nudism.

He defended anyone at war with the West, as Western laws allow. He prosecuted anyone protecting us, such as Dutch politician Geert Wilders. Agnostic and part Indonesian, Wilders called half the Koran fascist (without meaning to defend the other half). Spong had more reason than most people to fear sharia but, without any role in the case, intervened after the public prosecutor declined to prosecute Wilders. He invoked article 12 of the Criminal Code to obtain a court order forcing the prosecutor to prosecute Wilders for insulting Islam.

Jews have no greater friend on earth than Western nationalists, but can't see it. Muslim threats haven't diminished Jewish wariness of the West for perpetrating the Holocaust. We're Israel's best bastion beside its people, but remain a risk in Jewish eyes.

Still, all Spong had in mind for Wilders was criminal prosecution. It seemed fairly mild compared to the breaking news headlines on the *News Limited Network* website: 'Aussie cleric calls for MP's beheading.'

Now it was hard to imagine the Aussie cleric at our parish Anglican church, with his bright yellow braces, calling for someone's beheading. The headline referred instead to Sydney-born Feiz Mohamed. Refusing to discriminate between religions, we made him and our parish priest synonymous.

Of Wilders, Mohamed in a website chat room urged Muslims to "*chop off his head.*" A man comfortable with modern communications media, Mohamed's lectures had been included in a box of computer discs urging young Muslims to kill non-believers. He was equally comfortable before a crowd, having told an audience in Bankstown Town Hall five years earlier that women who were raped had only themselves to blame, because they dressed in "nothing but satanic skirts," teasing men's "carnal nature." At the time, he was head of the Global Islamic Youth Centre.

The news article mentioned a man prevented from entering Britain for spreading hatred and under trial in the Netherlands for inciting racial hatred, but the man wasn't Mohamed. It was Wilders.

We don't need to be lawyers to defend Muslims from

accusations of terrorism. The cancellation of a car race at Oakleigh in Melbourne the third Friday of March 2010 led to hundreds of rioters, described only as *"revheads,"* storming the streets. They smashed a Bob Jane T Mart tyre store, rolled over a car, and ignited flares. It was all unremarkable amidst multiculturalism, without mention of race or religion, until a rioter, Omar Amr, appeared outside court. His father, Gad Amr, pleaded with Channel Nine television cameraman Simon Fuller to stop filming them.

"I'm just doing my job, mate," replied Fuller.

"You bloody idiot," Omar Amr told the cameraman. "F*** off."

"The camera's rolling," replied Fuller.

"You idiot," added Gad Amr. "I don't care you say to whoever, you idiot."

"F*** him, mate," Omar Amr said to his father. "He's a f*** knuckle." (I don't know what that means.)

"You f***ing terrorist," replied Fuller.

No swearing or other abuse flying around, or even the cameraman's pestering, mattered as much as that word. Omar Amr confronted the Channel Nine crew. "Why are you calling him a terrorist?" Omar Amr demanded to know, referring to his father (although it appeared he'd been the one called a terrorist). "'Cos he has a beard and 'cos he's Muslim? It's what it comes down to? Is that what you guys have brung us down to? You can't even have a beard in this country anymore without being called a f***ing terrorist! Have some f***ing self-decency. The man has never been to court in his life, and you're calling him a terrorist!"

The cameraman apologised to the father and son. That wasn't enough. Channel Nine stood Fuller down pending an investigation.

Responses to the Twitter website were immediate, rebuking Fuller for his *"absolutely disgraceful behaviour."* People called him *"unprofessional,"* a *"massive scumbag,"* a *"f***ing coward"* (without the asterisks), and a *"pig."* Viewers felt *"sick,"* were left *"seething"* and *"infuriated,"* and hoped he'd *"never work again."* One said: *"Channel 9 must sack him immediately and issue public, grovelling apology."* A media worker was *"apalled & ashamed."*

The next night, Fuller was fired. There was no more word on Omar Amr, who'd been charged with incitement to riot, riot, affray, burglary, theft, and criminal damage in a Melbourne city street. Still, he wasn't to be called a terrorist.

The only moment we learnt the race or religion of any of the rioters that night in Melbourne was a religious slander making Muslims the victims. No amount of violence by other races or religions warrants us associating them with violence. Nothing prejudices our perceptions of others.

Bosnian Sulejman Talović came to America when he was ten years old, living in Utah where more than half the residents were members of the Church of Jesus Christ of Latter Day Saints. For motives that remained unclear, on the second Monday of February 2007, he murdered five bystanders in a normally peaceful Salt Lake City shopping mall. His religion might've remained a secret but for his Aunt Ajka, who assured the open-hearted people of Utah, "We are Muslims, but we are not terrorists."

We care little for white people suffering isolation and despair, injury and death. We care everything for what happens to everyone else, even if all they feel is offence.

In 2012, Gatwick airport guards detained war veteran David Jones (a creator of the children's character Fireman Sam) for an hour because of the threat not of terrorism but of prejudice. A Muslim woman had passed freely through airport security ahead of him without removing her scarf, when he joked with security staff, "If I was wearing this scarf over my face, I wonder what would happen." A Muslim security guard overheard and said she felt offended.

Humour is a dangerous weapon. Jones' passport and boarding pass were confiscated. Guards asked Jones, an elderly Englishman, how he'd feel to be labelled a "drunken old duffer?" Apparently that wasn't offensive.

Security staff, a British Airways manager, and a policeman tried to make Jones apologise. The policeman told him "that we now live in a different time and some things are not to be said."

"What I said had nothing to do with the woman's religion," Jones explained afterwards. "It was the fact that her face was covered and she seemed to have passed through that part of the security process without showing it." He was only allowed to leave when he agreed his remark *could* have been regarded as offensive.

England, Scotland, and Wales abolished blasphemy laws to accommodate religions other than Christianity. It would be quite ironic if we revived blasphemy laws to appease Islam.

12. OTHER PEOPLES' RIGHTS

The rights for which French revolutionaries butchered their aristocrats and each other from 1789 were for the French in the face of kings and governments. They weren't for everyone else. The new regime granted French Jews and French Africans rights, but passed a law in September 1793 ordering the arrest of all foreigners born in enemy countries and confiscation of their property.

Rights are powers a people earn or have conferred upon them. They're a Western invention grounded in nations: a Christian invention. That other races and religions don't think in such terms isn't the point. We do.

No longer reserving rights to our own, we insist upon everyone having rights Jews didn't have through the Holocaust. We deemed rights universal, granting them to the rest of the world, expecting nothing in return. They became everyone's rights: human rights. We deem them inalienable, as if we don't grant them: the ideology of rights. Entitlement became universal.

We plead for human rights everywhere, but only the West believes it. Western countries give more rights to everyone than other countries give anyone; minorities and majorities share an abundance of rights more than other countries give their majorities. None confer so many rights on so many as we do.

Most countries confer on their citizens some individual rights. What they give, they give only their people. They give foreigners few rights and revoke those rights without appeal when their people's interests require revocation. In effect, they confer only courtesies to foreigners, for as long as they choose.

In the world of comparative rights, we have fewer rights than other races do. They have our rights in our countries. We don't have their rights in theirs.

We value individuals, particularly individuals from outside our races. Other races value their communities more than individuals, particularly individuals from outside their races. Governments outside the West allow their people collective rights. People mightn't have the individual rights we demand for us all, but neither do people who'd harm them.

The absurdity of applying our values to others was never starker than in the case of French-born Moroccan Zacarias Moussaoui, involved in planning the September 2001 attacks. He was willing to be a suicide hijacker, but still we objected when an American court ruled him eligible for the death penalty. The jury sentenced him to life imprisonment.

Executing our compatriots legitimises killing, leading most Western countries to abolish the death penalty for even the most heinous of crimes. Refusing to discriminate, the bad things we abolished for our compatriots we abolished for everyone else.

Only Western countries don't make our people's lives paramount. "No one in this place would suggest that an Australian life is worth more than the life of someone from another country," weren't the words of an Afghan terrorist in the mountains. They were Australian parliamentarian Melissa Parke's words to parliament. No one questioned her presumption. "Yet if we have an inconsistent position on the death penalty when applied to Australians, as opposed to those from other countries, we leave ourselves open to this very criticism."

Undaunted by the injured and dead, Parke was arguing why Australia should press Indonesia not to execute the three terrorists we called the Bali bombers. Six years earlier, they'd killed two hundred and two people including eighty-eight Australians. Targeting nightclubs in the Kuta tourist district, the terrorists thought Australian lives were worth less than theirs. Theirs were the lives Parke wanted to save.

An international human rights lawyer, Parke had helped Kosovar Albanians and Palestinian Arabs. There are few surer signs of indifference to Western lives than the phrase "human rights" in a job description.

Chinese human rights activists fight for Chinese rights. Tibetan human rights activists fight for Tibetans' rights.

In Britain, the Islamic Human Rights Commission applauded a young Muslim woman working at a Heathrow airport kiosk after she wrote a poem 'How to Behead,' describing the slicing of hostages' heads. The British Court of Appeal agreed that encouraging terrorism wasn't a crime.

Human rights activists fight for their people's rights, unless they're Western. The Australian Human Rights Commission doesn't use images of terrorist victims in its campaigns. Its poster image became a beautiful Arab woman wearing a hijab. We fight for other races' rights; human rights are for their benefit, not ours.

Our preoccupation with rights reached its logical conclusion with Islamic war and terrorism. We refuse to discriminate, not anymore. It's unfair on the innocents and the guilty; they have rights, too. Terrorists are individuals with individual rights. Denying them their rights would be a crime and they become victims. If we have rights not to be victims, our rights don't matter.

There's no Human Rights Commission in Afghanistan. While we worry about Muslims feeling offended, the Taliban in June 2010 accused a seven-year-old boy of spying for America. It executed him.

A week later in Somalia, during the soccer World Cup in South Africa, the Hizbul Islam group killed two people watching a television broadcast of Nigeria playing Argentina. "We are warning all the youth of Somalia not to dare watch these World Cup matches," said Sheikh Mohamed Abdi Aros. "It is a waste of money and time, and they will not benefit anything or get any experience by watching mad men jumping up and down."

Our persisting fear of fascism leaves us suspicious not of Muslims but of our police and security forces, more fearful of them and their powers than of the people from whom they're trying to protect us. Fighting fascism, we make terrorists' civil liberties our own.

In a case brought by Kevin Gillan and Pennie Quinton, the European Court of Human Rights struck down section 44 of Britain's Terrorism Act 2000 allowing police to search people without reasonable suspicion of wrongdoing. Seven judges ruled unanimously that the searches could cause *"humiliation and embarrassment"* and breached the complainants' right to respect for their private lives under article 8 of the European Convention on Human Rights. Saving people's lives – our lives and certainly our compatriots' lives – were less important. We're better dead than rude.

If we'd fought World War II the way we fight Muslim terrorism, then Nazi Germany could have petitioned the High Court of Justice in London for an injunction against the Normandy landings. We'd apologise for any offence caused by the Dunkirk evacuation.

In 2015, our parish Anglican church treasurer James condemned suggestions the Australian government strip dual citizens fighting with Islamic State in the Middle East of their Australian citizenship for fear of what they might do if they returned to Australia. Those fighters didn't care. "*I have no concern if you cancel my passport*," declared physician Tareq Kamleh through the Facebook website. "*Do as you please, I no longer consider myself an Australian...*" The former womaniser and alcohol drinker had appeared in a propaganda film urging other medical professionals to join him aiding Islamic State.

In theory, we could care about each other as much as we care about people wanting to harm us. In practice, we don't want any hint of our old ways. When the rights of white people and other peoples diverge, the rights that come to the fore aren't ours; that would reek of old racism. The rights of some matter more than the rights of others. The rights of other races matter most.

From the moment Jordanian citizen Abu Qatada (otherwise known as Omar Othman) arrived in Britain on a false passport in 1993, he was "*heavily involved, indeed at the centre of terrorist activities associated with al-Qaeda.*" Official British documents described him as a "*truly dangerous individual*," advising and supporting the leader of the September 2001 hijackers and militant Islamic groups.

Even Muslim countries deal more harshly with Islamic threats and terror than we do. Twice, Jordanian courts convicted Qatada in his absence for conspiracy to bomb hotels in Amman in 1998 and for financing and advising a series of bombings in Jordan planned to coincide with the new millennium. A British appeals court spared sending Qatada back to Jordan not in spite of him being convicted of terrorism, but because he'd been convicted of terrorism. The British court felt those convictions meant he wouldn't get fair treatment in Jordan.

The Special Immigration Appeals Commission compelled the Ministry of Justice to release Qatada. He was subject to a twenty-two hour curfew at his west London home, electronically tagged, and barred from communicating with the head of al-Qaeda, among others.

That lasted six months before security concerns again led to Qatada being detained. A subsequent Law Lords' decision would have allowed his deportation to Jordan, before the European Court of Human Rights intervened.

"It makes a mockery of human rights law," complained parliamentarian Dominic Raab, "that a terrorist suspect deemed dangerous by our courts can't be returned home, not for fear that he might be tortured, but because European judges don't trust the Jordanian justice system." The Jordanians might use evidence obtained by torture against Qatada. In 2012, a British court again released him.

When Qatada's landlord became upset, the British government found Qatada, his wife, and their five children a new, larger home, funded by British taxpayers because he couldn't get a job. "Right now, he is the happiest man in Britain," said his brother Ibrahim Othman, as well he might.

No right is so destructive we don't allow it for others. Whatever the risk to Western lives, we don't subject foreign terrorists to foreign jurisdictions where they might be unfairly treated, not after refusing some Jewish refugees from Germany in the 1930s.

Bathing other races in rights so they can use them against us, they do. In 2005, the British government tried to evict an Algerian terrorist suspect, identified publicly only as T, who'd also entered Britain illegally. T used British legal recourse to remain in Britain, while under strict police surveillance costing a quarter of a million pounds per year. In 2010, the Special Immigration Appeals Commission allowed T to stay because, through the years T had been fighting deportation, his children had become accustomed to living in Britain.

We do all we can for other people's children. We're not so concerned for our own.

In 2009, my youngest daughter was a guest at Nicholas' fifth birthday party. Nicholas' father John was a New Zealander and his mother Irina a Russian, who'd met studying in Sweden. "They're the most diplomatic people," John said of the Swedes, "but they've ruined it letting in terrorists."

Never before had I heard of Sweden admitting terrorists. I'd heard only she accepted refugees.

"I'm not just saying that," explained John. "The Kurds, they know they're terrorists and I've met them." Swedes didn't like the way governments in countries like Turkey treated terrorists, so admitted them to Sweden. "They have guns under the tables."

John and I spoke of the irony of dictatorships like that in China defending their people. "Could you imagine our governments protecting us?" I asked him.

He practically laughed that I'd posed the question. "No!"

Australia didn't like the way China treated terrorists, so refused to return there Uighurs we knew to be terrorists. Terrorism qualifies them for refugee status.

In 2010, Australia's Refugee Review Tribunal granted asylum to a Palestinian Arab (who'd come to Australia two years earlier on a student visa) because of his links to the terrorist organisation Fatah al-Islam, linked in turn to al-Qaeda. "*In these circumstances, it cannot discount as remote or far fetched the possibility that he would be of adverse interest to the Lebanese security authorities, as a suspected member or supporter of FAI, should he return to Lebanon, and that he would, as a consequence, be arrested and detained, possibly for a lengthy period, without charge.*" (The acronym made Fatah al-Islam sound like an insurance company.)

"*The tribunal is satisfied that this persecution would be directed against the applicant because of a political opinion imputed to him, namely support for or membership of FAI.*" We'd made membership of a terrorist organisation and support for Islamic terrorism merely an imputed political opinion.

"*The tribunal is satisfied that the measures likely to be taken against the applicant are not justified by the fact that FAI is a designated terrorist organisation, which engages in acts of violence against the Lebanese state.*" We don't detain members of terrorist organisations committing acts of violence for lengthy periods without charge. We refuse to return them to countries that do.

Monash University researcher Greg Barton supported the decision because the Arab might've been coerced into joining Fatah al-Islam. "It's certainly reasonable to ask whether he poses a security risk," said Barton, "but at the same time we need to offer protection to those who need it."

We're the people needing protection. Australian intelligence agencies would monitor the Arab.

Western humanitarianism helps people who'd kill us. The Danish Security and Intelligence Service (*Politiets Efterretningstjeneste*) sought for more than a year to expel Iraqi Amer Saeed from Denmark for being a risk to Danish national security, believing him to be al-Qaeda's principal recruiter of suicide bombers in Northern Europe. It failed, in 2009, on supposedly humanitarian grounds.

It also sought to expel from Denmark his friend and fellow recruiter Mohamad Ezzedine Hamid. Again, it failed.

So little do we value each other and ourselves beneath our cavalcade of rights, we stand nobly estranged from the consequences. Giving everyone the full gamut of rights, uninterested in who benefits and who suffers, our introspective ideologies blind us to blood in London underground trains or on Moscow theatre seats. We divorce from our thinking our people who die.

Rights matter more than relationship. We're not deterred from helping others because those others might maim the woman and her baby at the end of our street. We don't countenance discrimination not even to save our brother from being assaulted or our daughter from being raped. If a terrorist's life is worth no less than our compatriots' lives, then it's worth no less than our children's lives. If we knew the victim would be us, we still wouldn't discriminate. We think all lives are equal, including our own.

Not even to save ourselves have we the mood to deny the rest of the world. That would be nationalism. If anything, endangering our lives makes us proud. We're happy to sacrifice white lives on humanitarian grounds.

If rights are worthwhile, they're in living freely among people at peace. Every right we possess only to the extent others don't erase it. Defending other people's liberties denies us ours. We don't need more rights we can't use, but more rights we can. If all that seems radical, then it's only radical in the West.

Personally, I respect other races for their loyalties. I have mine. I'd gladly surrender my freedoms if the people who'd harm my family and race also lost theirs. I'd entrust power to a government that stood on our side as I don't trust governments siding with others. Making our rights universal and inalienable hasn't brought us anything we didn't already have, or could've had, if we'd learn to cook foreign foods.

13. FREEDOM FROM SPEECH

Like Europe, French actress and beautiful blonde icon Brigitte Bardot grew old. By the age of seventy-three, she was suffering arthritis. Unlike Europe, she remained feisty, at least in her writing. Animals had long been her passion, and she campaigned vigorously for Muslims in France to stun animals before ritually slaughtering them. *"I've had enough of being led by the nose by this whole population which is destroying us,"* she complained in a letter to the interior minister, *"destroying our country by imposing their ways."*

We become upset whenever white people criticise other cultures. We become upset when animals are maltreated. The two sensitivities conflict wherever other cultures mistreat animals. Our rejection of prejudice normally prevails. In 2008, a French court fined Bardot fifteen thousand euros for writing that letter.

The fine was her fifth for inciting hatred against Muslims. *"I'm sickened by how"* French as much as Muslims *"are harassing me,"* she wrote to the court.

Their rights include freedom *from* speech: from hearing speech they dislike. Freedom *of* speech is theirs alone.

Bardot's case was a clear contrast with that of Mohamed Bourokba a few months later. For six years, his rap music accused French police of murdering hundreds of his brothers. French-born Bourokba's brothers weren't French. They were Algerians (like his parents who'd arrived in the 1960s) and other North Africans, wherever they were born.

Charged with public libel against the police, French courts twice acquitted Bourokba. When the Ministry of the Interior succeeded in having the case heard a third time, a third French court acquitted him.

Freedom of speech has become selective. We allow a young Algerian to accuse unabashed the French police of being racist mass murderers. We punish an elderly Frenchwoman complaining about other races imposing their cultures upon France.

"The college of Sliedrecht has a proposal to receive 250 refugees in the

coming 2 years," typed Mark Jongeneel, a small business owner in Sliedrecht, in Dutch on the Twitter website in January 2016. "*What a bad plan! #letusresist.*"

Dutch police visited his mother's home and then his place of work, warning him he would be responsible if there were riots like those in other towns protesting against immigrants. "You tweet a lot," police told him. "We have orders to ask you to watch your tone. Your tweets may seem seditious." Multiculturalism considers patriotism to be sedition.

Police also visited eight or nine people in Kaatsheuvel, which planned to house twelve hundred immigrants. Johan had typed into the Facebook website, "*we're not happy with the asylum seekers in our country.*"

The voices we're keen to hear aren't ours. In May 2009, illegal immigrants rioted in Athens after a policeman allegedly tore up a Koran while checking identity papers, but that wasn't a reason for Greeks to fret. It was a relief. Human rights activist Thanassis Kourkoulas enthused that illegal immigrants to Greece finally "have a voice."

We protest measures protecting us. Other races protest those obstructing them.

Immigrants haven't proven as tolerant of the West as the West is tolerant of immigrants. At their morning tea at the end of second term 2014, the women teaching Scripture at our local primary school felt Western women couldn't safely enter Muslim suburbs of Sydney.

Austrian Jewish philosopher Karl Popper wrote of the Intolerance Paradox in the first volume of his 1945 book *The Open Society and Its Enemies*. "*Unlimited tolerance must lead to the disappearance of tolerance. If we extend unlimited tolerance even to those who are intolerant, if we are not prepared to defend a tolerant society against the onslaught of the intolerant, then the tolerant will be destroyed, and tolerance with them.*"

In January 2013, the Muslim Patrol published a brief film on the YouTube website protesting advertisements for push-up bras by High Street retailer H&M in Britain. "The Muslims have taken it upon themselves to command the good and forbid the evil and cover up these naked people." Hooded men vandalised the advertisements, pouring petrol over one and igniting it.

Soon afterwards, the patrol published a three-minute film *The Truth About Saturday Night*, which came with the description: "*From women walking the street dressed like complete naked animals with no self-respect, to drunk people carrying alcohol, to drunks being killed in the middle of the road, we try our best to capture and forbid it all.*" It showed hooded Muslims forcing a passer-by to put away a can of lager, telling him that alcohol is a "forbidden evil," and telling a group of women "they need to forbid themselves from dressing like this and exposing themselves outside the mosque." When a young woman told them they were in Great Britain, they replied by saying "they don't respect those who disobey god."

None of their actions would've come to light, but for the Muslim Patrol advertising them. "We don't care if you are appalled at all," it said, "vigilantes implementing Islam upon your own necks."

A few days later, another short film showed the hooded Muslims harassing a homosexual man walking alone in Whitechapel. "Mate," one Muslim told him, "don't you know this is a Muslim area?"

"This is a Muslim area," shouted another Muslim, "get out of here. Get out here you bloody fag. You can't stay 'round here anymore."

"You are walking through a Muslim area dressed like a fag," said a Muslim. "You need to get out of here. Get out of here quicker. You're dirty mate."

"Are you dirty?" a Muslim demanded the homosexual admit. "Say it again."

Some people progress from ideology to reality, at least to some degree. A former communist, Dutch sociologist Pim Fortuyn saw the rise in violent crime in the Netherlands due to young Moroccans, Turks, and West Indians. He realised Muslim ghettoes in Rotterdam, Amsterdam, and The Hague refused assimilation into the Netherlands, threatening the country's liberal society and national cohesion. In 2002, he said the Netherlands, with one of the highest population densities in the world, was too crowded to accept more immigrants.

Fortuyn's Dutch supporters, particularly women, complained that Muslims looked derisively at them wearing clothes revealing their flesh. They spoke of being pressed to keep out of Muslim suburbs if they didn't dress and act in accordance with Muslim customs.

Otherwise, Fortuyn remained socially tolerant, but declared

there should be "no tolerance of the intolerant." (We say the same, but only of intolerant white people.) Fortuyn was also homosexual. "Why should I be tolerant of people who are not tolerant of me?" He called Islam a "backward culture."

Rotterdam police secretly investigated Fortuyn, finding no evidence of illegality. The law had failed.

The first Monday in May 2002, in a parking lot outside a radio station in Hilversum, Fortuyn was murdered, but not by an immigrant. Fellow Dutchman Volkert van der Graaf murdered him for making "scapegoats" of Muslims, whom van der Graaf thought were "the weak parts of" Dutch society. (An environmentalist and animal rights activist, van der Graaf was also upset by Fortuyn wanting to relax their country's prohibition on breeding animals for fur, a rare foray by Fortuyn into animal rights.)

Only after Fortuyn's death did police arrest the Dutchmen who, a few weeks earlier, had assaulted Fortuyn during a press conference. Until then, throwing a pie made from vomit and excrement had been lawful freedom of speech, when striking a person questioning Muslim immigration.

Fortuyn wasn't the only Dutchman to speak out of turn. Descended from painter Vincent van Gogh's brother was film director and writer Theo van Gogh. He was an atheist who, like other Europeans, enjoyed deriding Christianity. He called Jesus "the rotten fish of Nazareth."

Unlike other Europeans, van Gogh moved onto other religions. In 1991, he suggested Jews were unduly preoccupied with the Holocaust, almost half a century past. (So is the West.) In a magazine interview, he explained a "smell of caramel" by, referring to extermination camps, saying "today they're only burning diabetic Jews."

Following criticisms from Jewish historian Evelien Gans, van Gogh wrote in *Folia Civitatis* magazine that he suspected she "*gets wet dreams about*" sexual intercourse with Nazi physician Josef Mengele. Van Gogh wanted her to sue him so she would need to explain in a court of law why his remark was untrue.

Van Gogh's comments about Islam were relatively temperate. He further tempered that criticism by distinguishing Islam from political Islam seeking to impose sharia upon others, which he called an increasing threat to liberal Western societies. Had he been younger, he said he would've emigrated to America: a beacon of light in a darkening world. (Boy, would he have been in for a shock.)

Those thoughts were set out in a 2004 short film *Submission*, directed by him and written by Somali-born Ayaan Hirsi Ali, whom van Gogh had sponsored. She'd rejected Islam and become an atheist.

Muslims were furious. The son of Moroccan immigrants, Mohammed Bouyeri was born in Amsterdam in 1978 and enjoyed tertiary education for five years without graduating. His religion prevented him from serving alcohol at work or attending functions with women, but not from viewing pornography, especially amputee fetishes and necrophilia. He believed democracy violated Islam because only Allah could make laws. Armed jihad, he believed, was the only option for Muslims in the Netherlands.

While van Gogh was bicycling to work early the first Tuesday morning of November 2004, in front of the Amsterdam East borough office, Bouyeri fulfilled his Muslim duty. He shot van Gogh eight times with a handgun, stabbed him in the chest, cut his throat nearly decapitating him, and left two knives implanted in his torso, one attaching a five-page letter to his body. The letter, together with another he carried with him and others he'd written, complained that Jews dominated Dutch politics, pleaded for the destruction of America, Europe, and particularly the Netherlands, and threatened the life of Dutch nationalist Geert Wilders.

Dutch reaction was immediate. Rotterdam mayor Ivo Opstelten ordered the removal of Chris Ripken's mural of an angel with the words *"Thou shalt not kill"* outside his studio, because Muslims in a nearby mosque might feel offended.

Ayaan Hirsi Ali went into hiding. She still needs police protection, anywhere in the world.

The West lauds freedom of speech and our right to satirise religion, but our right to laugh is to laugh at our religion, not anyone else's. We have Jesus and Christians to mock.

Trey Parker and Matt Stone prided themselves offending just about everyone with their American animated television series *South Park*, until a 2010 episode portrayed the prophet Mohammed behind a bear costume. The American-based website *Revolution Muslim* warned Parker and Stone they could meet the same end as Theo Van Gogh.

The subsequent episode continuing that story deleted all

mention of Mohammed. A large block marked *"censored"* concealed the character. The episode was almost incomprehensible, but that wasn't the point. The sword had its reward.

For those threats against Parker and Stone, the *Revolution Muslim* site's founder, Jesse Curtis Morton, was jailed for twelve years. There followed a rare newspaper reference to a criminal being Muslim, although it was hard to imagine how the person behind such a site could be anything else. The *Sydney Morning Herald* newspaper carefully called him a Muslim convert, making him a little less Muslim, without mentioning what Morton called himself: Younus Abdullah Muhammed.

Muslim violence and threats of violence don't harm Islam. They help its cause. Not as brave as our forebears, our talk of tolerance belies the fact we're frightened. We worry about upsetting Muslims, but torment our own knowing they won't kill us in reply.

In September 2012, the French satirical magazine *Charlie Hebdo* published cartoons mocking Christianity and other religions, including Islam. It might have seemed we weathered that outrage from Muslims, but in January 2015, Muslim brothers Saïd and Chérif Kouachi forced their way into the *Charlie Hebdo* offices in Paris. There, they murdered twelve people and injured eleven, before fleeing.

Murdering magazine staff was not enough. Among other related attacks, heavily armed Amedy Coulibaly entered a kosher food supermarket in Porte de Vincennes. There, he murdered four Jewish hostages and held fifteen other Jews hostage, demanding that the Kouachi brothers not be harmed. The police ended the siege by storming the supermarket and killing Coulibaly.

The Kouachi brothers took hostages at a signage company in Dammartin-en-Goële. When they emerged from the building firing their weapons, police shot them dead.

Asserting the surviving cartoonists' rights of free speech without regard for the result, the *Charlie Hebdo* magazine published more cartoons picturing the prophet Mohammed. Without recognising race, religious differences, and other human interests, liberalism becomes another ideology stampeding over people, no less confrontational and provocative than any other.

Among Muslim protests worldwide against not the murders but the cartoons, killing ten people and burning forty-five churches in Niger, Muslims in Sydney planned a rally in Lakemba. With our usual understatement, a spokesman said New South Wales police would "not tolerate anyone who attempts to cause disharmony with any community."

Five years later, in October 2020, French school teacher Samuel Paty led a classroom discussion about freedom of speech in the town of Conflans-Sainte-Honorine. After inviting Muslim students to leave the classroom if they wished, he showed some of his teenage students a *Charlie Hebdo* cartoon, possibly two cartoons, depicting the prophet Mohammed.

In protest, Brahim Chnani, a parent of one of the pupils, spread word of Paty's actions. So did the Grande Mosque de Pantin in Paris.

Word reached eighteen-year-old Chechen refugee Abdullakh Anzorov, with no connection to the school. Twelve years earlier, France had welcomed Anzorov as a six-year-old refugee. A week and a half after Paty had shown the cartoon to the students, Anzorov waited at the school gates after school. Students pointed Paty out to Anzorov, who followed him a short way before beheading him in the street with a knife, shouting "*Allahu Akbar*."

"We will always defend freedom of expression," responded Canadian prime minister Justin Trudeau, "but freedom of expression is not without limits. We owe it to ourselves to act with respect for others and to seek not to arbitrarily or unnecessarily injure those with whom we are sharing a society and a planet."

In short, freedom of speech and other expression does not extend to anything that offends Muslims. It can only offend Christians.

The German people's traditional tolerance of Jews led to Germany having so numerous a Jewish population. Far from eradicating fascism, we are risking its renewal: laying the groundwork for a future fierce reaction by people braver or more desperate than we are, casting timidity aside.

We can't imagine anyone but white people being Nazis, but early in the twenty-first century, a handful of Nazi Jews arose in Israel responding to its racial minorities. There isn't such a risk in our other wartime foe: racially homogenous Japan.

In 2011, former Australian immigration minister Kevin Andrews said political leaders failing to speak out about the rise of extreme Islam contributed to the rise of nationalist movements. "What actually concerns me the most is that we can't have a discussion about it."

Another Liberal Party parliamentarian, Mitch Fifield, warned of "parallel societies" in Europe where Muslim groups preached sharia. "Australians certainly revel in diversity and embrace different cultures, but they expect everyone to integrate and sign up to mainstream values."

Senator Cory Bernardi warned of a growing "cultural divide" in Australia, with a Melbourne university reserving toilets for Muslims. "I, for one," he said, referring to the halal method of slaughtering meat, "don't want to eat meat butchered in the name of an ideology that is mired in sixth-century brutality and is anathema to my own values." The country should act "before it is too late."

The government's parliamentary secretary on immigration Kate Lundy fobbed off the fears. "The Australian community is uniquely diverse and we have a proud record of successfully leveraging the benefits of migration," she said. It was the language of commerce.

The only Muslim parliamentarian, Ed Husic, said the Liberal Party leader should end the "extremism" and "subterranean contest." He wasn't talking about Muslims, but about politicians.

The greatest condemnation of those warnings from Liberal Party politicians came from within the Liberal Party. Shadow attorney general George Brandis compared the comments to bullies beating up Italian schoolchildren in the 1960s. "It was from that experience that I formed my lifelong detestation of bullies who pick on a vulnerable minority just because they are different," he said. "Those of us from both sides of politics, who have championed the idea of a liberal society receptive to and respectful of people of all races and faiths, should resist those intemperate voices and be steadfast in its defence."

We refuse to imagine concern about other races and religions being anything but a fear of difference. Brandis spoke as if Muslims were like Italians, adults were children, and discussion amounted to bullying.

Greens immigration spokeswoman Sarah Hanson-Young called on her fellow parliamentarians to focus on positive aspects of an ethnic mix. Put another way, we should think only good things about other races and cultures. (We don't do the same about us and our cultures.)

We funnel everything bad done by Muslims in the name of

Islam away from Islam into something else. Anything good they do, or might have done, we credit to them.

The West's approach throughout our multicultural experiment has been to ignore the bad and find something good we think comes of it. That usually means restaurants. Dismissing the sacrifices our forebears suffered in war and the lives of our compatriots and descendants, we enthuse for rapidly growing Muslim populations because at some point in our lives, we might want a kebab.

14. INTEGRATION

In 1976, Australia accepted four thousand Lebanese immigrants. Furthermore, the Lebanese civil war led the Australian government to relax the eligibility criteria for admission of what senior public servants considered unskilled illiterate refugees of questionable characters and standards of personal hygiene.

The government also operated a family reunion scheme, which allowed no end of relatives to follow one immigrant into the country. Whole villages reputedly transposed from Lebanon to Sydney suburbs. Prime Minister Malcolm Fraser cared far more about foreign families being together than he ever cared about Australian families, although having their relatives nearby hadn't deterred them when they emigrated in the first place, unless the plan was always to bring the daisy chain of cousin onto cousin. We recognise extended families and clans in others, we no longer recognise in ourselves.

Cabinet papers remain secret for thirty years, when the National Archives generally releases them. Unknown to the Australian public until 2007, senior public servants in 1976 warned the government not to accept Muslim refugees they said would never integrate into Australian society. Multiculturalist Fraser, whose maternal grandfather was Jewish, fobbed off the warnings.

Confronted in 2007 with reports of those warnings after Lebanese had recently rioted in Sydney, Fraser believed Muslim youth felt alienated from Australian society because Australian governments had failed to integrate them into what he called the general community, as if there were still such a thing. More than any prime minister beforehand, Fraser ended the sense of there being a general community.

We're too individualistic to integrate with each other, but have embraced Muslims like other immigrants. At law school, we did not contradict Sunalp; nobody mentioned Armenians. My youngest sister accompanied him to the College of Law ball in 1986.

We imagine people of other races and religions all being like our friends among them. They're not. Sometimes, our friends are not.

Also in 1986, Irishwoman Anne-Marie Murphy must have thought she had a good relationship with her Jordanian fiancé, Nezar Hindawi. He told her he wanted her to meet his parents before marriage so, five months pregnant, she prepared to board the El Al airlines flight from Heathrow to Tel Aviv the penultimate Thursday morning of April. He wasn't flying with her, but had given her a bag to carry with her. Until Israeli security guards inspected it, she didn't know the bag contained one and a half kilograms of Semtex explosives.

Hindawi hadn't meant anything personal towards her and their child. He just wanted to kill the three hundred and seventy-five passengers aboard an Israeli aircraft.

It's hard to know what more Western governments or people could have done to welcome immigrants. My Polish friend Gerard was a teacher at Kingsgrove High School in Sydney for several years through 2006, but teaching Muslim children was difficult because their parents taught them non-Muslims were inferior.

We could be of some use: a Muslim Lebanese father called on teachers to help find his daughter. Standing amidst them in their common room when a telephone call told them they'd located the girl in the company of a friend, he grabbed the handset and screamed at her: "Is she an Aussie? I told you not to associate with Aussies!"

Immigrants aren't Australians, in his view. In our view, they are.

A 2009 newspaper headline 'Aussie mother jailed two years for 'insulting' Kuwaiti emir' referred to Kuwaiti-born Nasrah Alshamery, who immigrated to Australia a decade earlier. She mightn't have called herself an Aussie mother, but we did. We made her indistinguishable from our mothers, however unlikely our mothers were to insult anyone, with or without quotation marks.

Kuwait (which Western countries liberated from Iraq in 1991) hadn't integrated the Alshamerys or any others among the hundred thousand stateless Bidoons. It refused those fellow Arabs rights to work.

Australia gave the Alshamerys the right to work, although they didn't exercise it. Nasrah Alshamery had seven children and, not for that reason, was on an Australian disability pension. Her husband enjoyed carer's benefits to look after her. None of her alleged health problems, which included type 2 diabetes, lower-back problems, and depression, kept them from holidaying in Kuwait.

The more I read, the more I understood Kuwait not wanting the Alshamerys, but we weren't about to refuse them. I could only surmise what made them choose to live in Australia, although the disability and carer's pensions were a pretty good starting point. I had trouble wondering what benefit they brought to Australia, although I knew we'd insist they brought something.

What might've been the only time we refused the Alshamerys anything, the Australian government refused to intervene in Kuwaiti legal process after Nasrah Alshamery insulted the Kuwaiti emir. I can't imagine how the Australian government could intervene. It didn't matter that no other people, not even their own, gave the Alshamerys what we gave them. Not getting everything they wanted made them angry.

Soltan Ahmad Azizi thought we'd done too much to integrate Muslims. Two years after Australia admitted him and his wife Marzieh Rahimi as Afghan refugees in 2005, he complained that the mother of his five children was "too Australian," after she complained about his violence and wanted a divorce. He strangled her with her veil.

Judge Betty King's most public criticism at Azizi's trial wasn't of Muslims, refugees, or other immigrants. She "*slammed*" the emergency services operator who'd called the police after Rahimi telephoned for help, for not also obtaining an interpreter.

America also sought to integrate her immigrants, but in 2006, Ihsan Bagby of the Council on America–Islamic Relations' Washington office said that Muslims "can never be full citizens… because there is no way we can be fully committed to the institutions and ideologies of this country." Among America's ideologies is multiculturalism.

In 2009, more than a decade after he'd arrived in America, Faleh Hassan Almaleki of Glendale, Arizona complained that his daughter Noor Faleh Almaleki wasn't living by traditional Iraqi values. He thus drove a car over her.

Canada was doing more than most Western countries to recognise sharia. Authorities in Ontario were nevertheless unaware Mohammad Shafia was in a polygamous marriage with Zainab Shafia and Tooba Mahommad Yahya until 2009, when he, his second wife, and their son Hamed murdered his childless first wife and three daughters to restore the family honour. The daughters had brought dishonour by having boyfriends and wearing revealing clothes.

Thinly veiled rebukes of white racism shone from the 2010 film of the first part of *Harry Potter and the Deathly Hallows* and other Harry Potter films, in which young actress Afshan Azad played the role of Padma Patil. Azad, her older brother Ashraf, and their parents weren't any less Bangladeshi for having all been born in England. When Ashraf caught her at their home in Longsight, Manchester speaking on the telephone to her Hindu boyfriend in May 2010, he punched her, dragged her around by her hair, and strangled her. Her three-hour ordeal also involved her parents, through which she was called a "slag" and "prostitute" and told: "Marry a Muslim or you die!"

It caused her swelling, grazes, and bruises around her eyes, face, left ear, forehead, and forearms, but the prosecution accepted that Ashraf and his father hadn't threatened to kill her. The defence lawyer blamed Ashraf's actions on having drunk alcohol. Other Muslim wives and children are presumably more obedient to their husbands and fathers.

In 2009, Muslim boys at Punchbowl Public School bullied eleven-year-old Antonios Grigoriou for eating a salami sandwich during the Muslim fasting month of Ramadan. A Muslim student punched him in the eye and kicked his legs, forcing his mother to withdraw him from the school. "He has been bullied from day one... about being a Christian and about the hot salami in his lunch," said his mother. "My boy has a Greek background... the bullying is extreme. He has been called a fat pig, and hit on the back with a stick."

The Department of Education and Training had a zero-tolerance policy towards racism. ("Zero tolerance" is one of our favourite phrases, even for dealing with intolerance.) "Claims of bullying or racial intolerance are taken very seriously and looked into," said a department spokeswoman. "The school education director is looking into the matter and called the father concerned. As a result... the school will work with all families and students involved to ensure that the values promoted by Punchbowl Public School and the department are understood and supported."

The school suspended the Muslim student described as "the ringleader of the group." It had "on-going cultural and interfaith awareness programmes to improve understanding among students of events like Ramadan and Christmas." (That was more than our children received at their schools, at least about Christmas.)

"Fundamentalists do not want integration," Somali-born Ayaan Hirsi Ali said of Muslims in 2010. "They teach young people that democracy, free thinking, is bad."

Not that the West still believes in free thinking. Democracy is becoming problematic.

Nevertheless, we reject any notion that races clustering together, failing to assimilate, can be anything but a failure of government policy or a result of racism: not theirs, but ours. "I won't say it happens on a daily basis," claimed Mohammed El-Leissy, a youth worker for the Victorian Islamic Council, in 2011, "but we do get calls from people saying, 'My wife or I have been spat on or verbally abused at the supermarket'."

He didn't identify those people, so far as I read. Asking him to provide corroborating evidence would be disrespectful.

Melbourne parliamentarian Kelvin Thomson said Australian governments had worked hard through recent decades to eliminate racism. They certainly had, if only by Australians. The National Anti-Racism Partnership and Strategy wasn't concerned about racism by immigrants.

In 2012, the Islamic Women's Welfare Association said Muslims prefer to be with their own. Australia should thus consider how to *"facilitate the purchase of homes for new migrants,"* it told an Australian government inquiry into multiculturalism. *"Migrants face a lot of sacrifices such as having to travel long distances to visit relatives, spending on communication costs, missing out on some events occurring in native countries etc. This loss should be compensated by the Government in one way or the other..."* The more we give immigrants, the more they want.

Employed by the insurance broker servicing Cement Australia, Steve described to his colleague Mario and me how little Muslims cared what we thought of them. In a past job as an investigator, Steve was interviewing a Muslim Arab woman about her fraudulent insurance claim. Her fraud had been obvious, but she'd assumed white people were easily duped. (For the most part, she was right.) Sitting before him, she leant to one side and loudly broke wind. When Steve confronted her with her fraud, she shrugged her shoulders.

In 2009, the *Sydney Morning Herald* newspaper reported wars between motorcycle gangs in Sydney. The headline referred only to a religious divide, but the article spoke of Sunni Muslims predominantly in west and south-western Sydney and Shi'ite Muslims predominantly in the St George area. We imagine Muslims coexisting peacefully with other religions, but they can't peacefully coexist with each other.

Gang members denied religion had anything to do with the warfare. The newspaper report the next day made no mention of Muslims, Sunni or Shi'ite. It just mentioned four *"people of the Islamic faith,"* which made them sound like any other category of faithful.

Several weeks later, a motorcycle gang member was murdered in Sydney airport. The dead man's brother, a prisoner in gaol, vowed revenge. News reports made no mention of race or religion, although the dead man's funeral was at a mosque.

By 2010, Middle Eastern gangs had expanded from Sydney to Queensland. Operating on the Gold Coast was the Sons of Islam or Soldiers of Islam, including former Iraqi soldiers with weapons training. (Soldiers from a country against which we went to war and from which we'd only withdrawn a year earlier are free to come here to live. Anything else would be racist.) In one member's home, police found pictures of terrorist leader Osama bin Laden.

Outlaw gangs don't confine themselves to fighting each other. Delays in his wife receiving haemorrhoid surgery from Gold Coast Hospital led Richard Savage (whose name belied his Middle Eastern descent) to a violent rampage, telling frightened nurses he was "the king of the Gold Coast." He threatened to get thirty Finks motorcyclists to wreck the hospital if his wife wasn't immediately operated upon.

15. RACE

Sometime through the 1990s, my Jewish friend Ian Biner told me he didn't like Germans, amidst a conversation in which he said his Danish girlfriend also didn't like Germans. I don't know if she was Jewish, but she was his girlfriend.

In all other respects, Ian passionately opposed racial or religious prejudice. "Everyone's the same," he said, dismayed when the people of Camden wanted to stop a Muslim school being built there. He alone suggested Holyman Limited set the date of an annual general meeting away from Jewish and Muslim holy days. (I was unaware of any Muslim shareholders, while the Welsh-born chief executive was as indifferent to Jewish holy days as he was to Christian ones, unless they were also public holidays.)

It took a while, but eventually Islamic terror affected Ian's attitude to Muslims. Russia's best known experience of Islamic terror was forty to fifty armed Chechens seizing the crowded Dubrovka Theatre on the penultimate Wednesday of October 2002, leading to a hundred and twenty-nine theatregoers dying and seven hundred being injured. Ian told me a Russian explained his country's fears by showing a visitor a huge crater in Moscow, where the population was more than ten million at the time. The crater was formed by Muslims attempting to detonate a nuclear bomb.

A Monday evening in September 2009, I was one of twelve people eating dinner at the Food and Plonk restaurant, Lindfield. The talk was of terror and al-Qaeda trying to get weapons of mass destruction, which it would surely try to use to murder millions of people. The only coloured person in the room was a Chinese man, a little older than I was. To have been at that dinner among political party selectors, he must've been an Australian citizen. A rare time he spoke was to refer us to what he called "the three real issues" of terrorism. "One," he said, stretching out a single finger to make his point, "race."

No one else spoke. It was a word, an idea, no one else

mentioned. The West had long learnt not to think of race, except to shame us.

"Two," he continued, his fingers outstretched, "religion."

Again, the rest of us said nothing. We didn't think as he thought, but were too polite to say so.

"Three," he finished, stretching his third finger into the air, "the haves and have-nots."

Conversation burst forth; we all presumed he meant having and not having money. Much as we'd spent decades blaming crime on economic disparities, we did the same for terrorism.

We thought ending poverty would defeat terrorism, in spite of Osama bin Laden being a billionaire's son and so many terrorists around the West coming from wealthy, or at least financially comfortable, families. Rich Saudis and other Muslims rewarded Iraqis who'd killed Western troops in Iraq and gave money to the impoverished families of Palestinian suicide bombers who'd killed Jews in Israeli streets and pizza parlours. It was capitalist-style reward and incentive, depending upon the bombers' sense of family over individualism.

The West works hard to find root causes of terrorism other than race or religion. The more we're attacked, the harder we try.

We think employment alleviates terrorism, but employment didn't deter a Bangladeshi employee of British Airways, Rajib Karim, from conspiring with American-born cleric Anwar al-Awlaki to plan an attack on an American-bound aircraft in 2010. Al-Awlaki had previously released a film urging Muslims to murder Americans. (Murdering passengers and crew wasn't part of the British Airways policy manual.)

Three years earlier, Karim joined the airline to carry out terrorism. We presume different races and cultures living and working together coalesce, but Karim wrote to his brother he had no doubts "*whatsoever*" that the people around whom he lived and worked were legitimate targets for attack. "*And the more I am mixing with them, the more my conviction is getting stronger.*"

Karim wasn't the first airline or airport employee convicted of terrorism. Russell Defreitas, one of the men convicted for a failed 2007 plot to bomb John F Kennedy International Airport in New York, was previously employed by Evergreen airlines. In February 2010, airport shuttle bus driver Najibullah Zazi pleaded guilty to three terrorism charges for conspiring to detonate an explosive in the New York City subway system.

Along with economic considerations, we assume education can make people whatever we want them to be; it does with our children. On Christmas Day 2009, Nigerian student Umar Farouk Abdulmutallab of University College London tried to blow himself up on an aeroplane flight to Detroit.

Andrew Zammit of the Global Terrorism Research Centre at Monash University found that six in ten people facing terrorism charges in Australia up to 2012 and twenty of the thirty-three alleged jihadists in Australia since 2001 were Muslims of Lebanese descent, a phenomenon unique to Australia. At least a further sixteen other Australian citizens were arrested in Lebanon for alleged terrorist activity. Sam Mullins, a research fellow at the Centre for Transnational Crime Prevention at Wollongong University, said it reflected Australia's immigration history. (Most Australian Muslims then were Lebanese.)

When Melbourne police arrested four men plotting a suicide attack on an Australian Army base in 2009, the first newspaper headline spoke only of them being extremists. In one of the most bizarre turns of illogic I'd read, journalist Paul Colgan argued the arrests were evidence that racial profiling was useless in the hunt for criminals because, he wrote, without any obvious sense of what he was saying, they were *"Australian nationals of Somali and Lebanese background."*

The terrorists weren't of one race. They were of two.

For the West, citizenship is at the fore and race in the background. It's hard to imagine people planning to blow up an Australian Army base feeling that way.

If it seemed spurious to think racial profiling is useless because terrorists could come from two races, Colgan went onto argue that terrorists could be *"younger and older Indonesian Muslims (Jemaah Islamiah), East Africans (al-Shabaab), Lebanese and other Eastern Mediterraneans (Hezbollah and al-Shabaab), young Middle-Eastern Muslims (al-Qaida), young Pakistanis (Lashkar-e-Toiba) and lost, young white Australians like David Hicks or Shane Kent (potentially any of the above)."*

Not that I understood the distinction between being Lebanese, Eastern Mediterranean, and Middle Eastern, although only the latter Colgan mentioned being Muslim. He seemed concerned that we imagine Indonesians and Middle Easterners who aren't Muslims could be terrorists.

I had to research to discover who Shane Kent was. Colgan omitted to mention that he and Hicks had converted to Islam. Colgan seemed not to understand the racial profiling inherent in realising that white people becoming terrorists were lost, as Muslims from other races weren't.

Colgan wasn't the only advocate for immigrants who said much that he didn't mean to say. Reported with those arrests (as I'd not previously seen reported) was an old warning by a Somali community leader in Sydney, Herse Hilole, that young Somali refugees in Melbourne were returning to Somalia to fight and could be recruited for attacks in Australia.

Accepting Somali refugees brought those terrorists to Australia, but that didn't deter us from welcoming more. Colgan noted that plenty of terrorists weren't from Somalia.

We don't link race to terrorism. We only link race to measures defending us from terrorism.

In America, the Minority Business Development Agency helped entrepreneurs gain access to capital, contracts, and trade opportunities, provided they were from a supposedly disadvantaged race: African Americans, Puerto Ricans, Spanish speakers, American Indians, Eskimos, Aleuts, Hasidic Jews, Asian-Pacific Americans, and Asian Indians. In 2012, the Department of Commerce considered extending that special assistance to any *"American who traces his or her ethnic roots to one of the countries in the Arab World, including Algeria, Bahrain, Djibouti, Egypt, Iraq, Jordan, Kuwait, Lebanon, Libya, Mauritania, Morocco, Oman, Qatar, Somalia, Saudi Arabia, Sudan, Syria, Tunisia, United Arab Emirates, and Yemen,"* as well as Palestinians.

It followed a petition from the American Arab Anti-Discrimination Committee, which promoted discrimination for Arabs but opposed discrimination against them, namely *"discrimination and prejudice in American society resulting in conditions under which Arab American individuals have been unable to compete in a business world."* It highlighted the National Security Entry Exit Registration System, *"which required non-immigrants to register at ports of entry and targeted males from Arab nations; stricter travel guidelines; and 'no-fly lists' that predominantly contained the names of Arab Americans."* The petition claimed studies indicated that Arab Americans' earnings had fallen since the terrorist attacks of 2001 compared to other ethnic groups, that they'd been subject to harassment and racial profiling while receiving *"few prime government contracts,"* and that *"in the government's efforts to protect Americans, they essentially took away the rights of other Americans."*

In April 2013, a bomb killed three people (including eight-year-old Martin Richard) and injured approximately two hundred and sixty others at the Boston Marathon. Fearing that immigration might be affected or Muslims subjected to more scrutiny if the bomber turned out to be Muslim, commentator David Sirota hoped the bomber proved to be a white American. He blamed white privilege for white American killers being treated as lone wolves, while Islamists were considered an existential threat.

Yet, white killers generally acted alone; that is individualism. Muslim terrorists enjoyed communities and often organisations, as races other than ours do.

Sirota's critics were equally jaundiced about race. They called him a white male, even a liberal, instead of noticing he was Jewish. He knew the existential threat white people were.

Sirota would be disappointed. There proved to be two bombers: Muslim Chechen brothers Tamerlan and Dzhokhar Tsarnaev. The racists were right.

Born in Kyrgyzstan before moving to Russia, their father brought them to America on a ninety-day tourist visa in 2002 before claiming to have been persecuted in Russia for being Chechen. Instead of suggesting they return to Kyrgyzstan, America granted the parents and four children asylum and later refugee status. Tamerlan married a woman who converted to Islam and they bore a child. The beneficiary of a City of Cambridge scholarship, Dzhokhar became an American citizen on the eleventh of September 2012. Their father returned to Russia (presumably without fear of persecution), while the brothers collected a hundred thousand dollars in government benefits.

They'd been Boston's multicultural dream, before willing to become martyrs in paradise; the generosities America accorded them meant nothing. A few days after the bombing, they ambushed and murdered a policeman. They forced another man to drive around Boston while they bragged about the bombing, before engaging in a gun battle with police. While hiding in a boat before being captured, Dzhokhar Tsarnaev wrote: *"When you attack one Muslim, you attack all Muslims."* That's nationalism.

When you attack a white person, she's on her own. That's

individualism.

News reports of the night included images of a dark Mercedes car boot with Massachusetts registration plates and bearing a sticker spelling the word "*Coexist*" from religious symbols including the Islamic crescent, Star of David, and Christian Cross for three of the letters. Mere coexistence side by side is a weak vision for a place, but we'd given up on community.

Another Coexist sticker appeared on a car in comfortable Sydney suburban Roseville three days before Christmas that year. We imagine creating the world we want with stickers.

Other races don't. Muslims believe religious coexistence denies the sovereignty of Allah.

In February 2015, French artist Combo painted the word "*coexist*" on a wall in Porte Dorée, Paris using an Islamic crescent, Star of David, and Christian Cross. Four Muslims told him the painting was very offensive and demanded he remove it. When he refused, they beat him, leaving him with a dislocated shoulder, bruises, and a black eye. *Le Monde* newspaper reported the assailants as merely four young men.

The artist refused to discuss his assailants' identities. "It would only add fuel to the fire," he said. Even after being bashed, we refuse to encourage prejudice against other races and religions.

Never have I read of racism as irrational as the West's fanatical rejection of racism. Sweden denied Rakhmat Akilov's claim for asylum in 2016, ordering him to leave the country, but he remained. The first Friday in April 2017, the Muslim Uzbek hijacked a truck and drove it into a Stockholm crowd. Among the four dead was eleven-year-old Swedish girl Ebba Åkerlund and Belgian psychologist Maïlys Dereymaeker, aged thirty-one, who'd helped asylum seekers. In what euphemistically became known as the "Stockholm truck attack," Akilov said afterwards he'd deliberately targeted children. That Sunday, Swedes protested not against terrorism, immigration, or multiculturalism but the racism they feared the attack might encourage among Swedes.

Our priorities were very clear with contrasting news reports of two horrific killings in Europe, the second Tuesday of December 2011. In Liege, convicted drug trafficker, weapons offender, and recipient of stolen goods Nordine Amrani threw three hand grenades and used an automatic rifle to shoot shoppers in a crowded market square, killing four people and wounding a hundred and twenty-three others before killing himself. The victims included two teenage boys just out of examinations and a seventeen-month-old girl. Their races and religions weren't mentioned, as Amrani's was not, although prosecutor Danièle Reynders made a point of telling a news conference: "He has no history of terrorist acts."

Websites like *Anorak* from Britain were adamant the Belgian-born Amrani had no links to terrorist groups, letting slip he was racially Moroccan. He was a criminal, not a terrorist, and everything was fine. Indeed, he'd been summoned to appear before police that morning on criminal matters. Ahead of the attack in St Lambert Square, he murdered a neighbour's cleaning lady.

That same day in Florence, writer Gianluca Casseri killed two street sellers before killing himself. News reports widely identified Casseri as Italian, his victims as Senegalese, and the crime as a racist killing. The *Sydney Morning Herald* newspaper headline described Casseri as a *"Racist Author."*

Dozens of Africans marched through Florence, pushing over parked motor scooters and garbage bins demanding justice. "Don't tell me he was crazy," one African told Italian news service *Ansa*, "because if he were crazy he would have killed both blacks and whites." It was a fascinating line.

16. RELIGION

A 2007 report from the Pew Research Centre found that seven percent of American Muslims aged between eighteen and twenty-nine had favourable opinions of the al-Qaeda terrorist organisation. While we imagine new generations becoming like us, young American Muslims were twice as likely as older Muslims to believe the name of Islam warranted suicide bombings.

Muslims don't suffer because of crime and terrorism. We do more to help them, without thought of what rich Muslims are doing. Under the Building Community Resilience programme of 2011, the Australian government awarded grants of up to a hundred thousand dollars each to Muslim community groups. "The new programme will focus on activities that support individuals away from intolerant and radical ideologies and encourage positive participation in the community," explained attorney general Robert McClelland.

In 2011, Monash University doctoral candidate Rachel Woodlock blamed Islamic radicalism on social exclusion, but not by Muslims: by us. She argued that *"most Muslims can buttress themselves against prejudice, seeking support through various sources of well-being, a minority will seek maladapted solutions. Some turn to gangs and criminality; a small number will join militant religious groups that provide them with a sense of connection and identity."* She pointed out that militant Muslims aren't particularly religious before becoming radical, but *"they belong neither to their parents' devout traditional cultures, nor to their Western host nations, which sends the message: Muslims don't belong."*

Her words acknowledged that multiculturalism inevitably fails, but life being hard for immigrant races isn't reason for us to withdraw our invitation. It's reason for us to try harder. Our white people's burden is to make multiculturalism work. It's our fault that it doesn't. The problem, argued Woodlock, is our *"anti-Muslim paranoia."*

She wanted *"facilitating the settlement and integration of Islam and*

Muslims in Australian society. It is precisely because Islam is not inherently violent, as is demonstrated by the productive and peaceful lives that the vast majority of Australia's 340,000 Muslims pursue, that permitting them to build and maintain the infrastructure of their communities – mosques, schools and businesses – alongside other religious and secular groups, will provide protection against violent extremism."

We'd done that, although no one can build whatever he likes wherever she likes. (It's hard enough to get council permission to cut down a tree.)

With a British general election leading to a new government, I often read and watched British news in May 2010. In Australia, journalist Mike Sullivan's report of an attack on British parliamentarian Stephen Timms in London was headed 'British politician stabbed in the stomach as he meets female constituent.' (We identify attackers by their gender, but not their race or religion.) We'd become so blasé about crime, it soon slipped my mind, until I read a second version of the story credited to Sullivan in the *Sun* newspaper in Britain, headed 'Woman in a veil knifed MP in gut.'

Veils could've led foolish readers to presume the assailant was Muslim. She might've been Christian, wearing a wedding veil.

The Sun could be indiscreet, mentioning that the assailant was Asian wearing an orange headscarf and veil, without suggesting the scarf and veil were Islamic. To prevent anyone being moved to think poorly of Asians, liking them any less, the article quoted local community worker Rahman Fazlur to say Timms, a faithful Christian, had *"first-rate relations with the Asian community."* It hadn't helped.

By 2016, our explanation for Muslims murdering strangers, such as Zakaria Bulhan murdering American woman Diane Horton and wounding five others in busy Russell Square, London in August, was that the killers suffered from mental illness. *"Authorities have ascribed jihad terror to mental illness on numerous occasions,"* wrote jihad expert Robert Spencer, regarding *"this curious epidemic of mental illness among Muslims?"* We could conceive no other explanation, unwilling to consider race or religion being relevant.

"His mental health problems are a scapegoat," said Bulhan's neighbour Parmjit Singh. "They said he had mental health issues, but that was not the boy I knew."

Bulhan was a devout Muslim. "Where does radical Islam end

and mental illness begin?" asked David Kupelian, author of *The Marketing of Evil: How Radicals, Elitists, and Pseudo-Experts Sell us Corruption Disguised as Freedom*, "and what if they are the same thing?"

G.M. Davis, author of *House of War: Islam's Jihad Against the World*, suggested the "brainwashed multicultural West" can't comprehend anything but tolerance. The violent nature of Islam was common knowledge, he said, until multiculturalism prohibited candour, honesty, and meaningful discourse in the West about race, religion, and more.

White racists, like South Carolina gunman Dylann Roof in 2015, have no excuses. "Pundit after pundit ignored the fact that Roof might also have been a truly mentally disturbed person," said pastor Carl Gallups.

I've never heard mention of a conference examining Muslim crime or terror, although I imagine any such conference would blame white people's prejudices. I've only found reference to conferences about crime, abuse, and attacks *upon* Muslims. In August 2015, the *Australian Broadcasting Corporation News* reported a conference in Melbourne about so-called Islamophobia. A Muslim woman claimed she suffered because of racism.

In May 2016, Greater Manchester Police prepared officers for terrorist attacks like those that had recently killed and injured hundreds of people in Paris and Brussels. Like those terrorists, the mock suicide bomber screamed "*Allahu Akbar*!"

"*Stupid decision by @gmpolice to decide attackers should be seen as Muslim*," responded Manchester University diversity officer Ilyas Nagdee through the Twitter website, among the rush of criticism. "*Maybe that's why Islamophobias gone up 300% in the UK.*" (Nagdee seems to have presumed Islamic terror had nothing to do with the increase.)

Manchester Police promptly apologised. "*Maybe in future training*," suggested L.P. Valentine, "*the suicide bomber could shout 'I'm blowing myself up for a generic terrorist cause'.*"

At the time of the 2001 terrorist attacks, there were twelve hundred mosques in America. The number almost doubled through the following ten years.

Little wonder plans unfolded in 2010 to build a hundred-million-dollar, thirteen-storey Muslim centre, including a five-hundred-seat auditorium, swimming pool, and mosque just two blocks away from what had been the World Trade Centre, New York. Ostensibly on aesthetic grounds but with full knowledge of the consequences, the Landmarks Preservation Commission voted unanimously to end the historic protection of the Italian Renaissance Palazzo-style former Burlington Coat building on Park Place. What had been a site of American manufacturing would become another symbol of American inclusion.

"We are Americans," said Sharif El-Gamal, chief executive of project developer SoHo Properties, "Muslim Americans."

Jewish mayor Michael Bloomberg said "we would betray our values if we treated Muslims differently than anyone else." Thus, the families of the dead should welcome the Muslim centre. "We do not honour their lives by denying the very constitutional rights they died protecting. We honour their lives by defending those rights and the freedoms the terrorists attacked."

I struggled to imagine those office personnel dying at their desks their last Tuesday morning with thoughts of Muslims' or anyone else's constitutional rights. We'd redefined the reasons our forebears went to war. We redefined reasons the victims of Muslim terrorism went to work.

More fury came from Muslims at Americans questioning the building of the Muslim centre than had come from Americans at Muslims for the 2001 attacks. "Rejecting this has become like rejecting Islam itself," declared Ahmad Moussalli, a professor of Islamic studies at the American University of Beirut. "The U.S. has historically been distinguished by its tolerance, whereas Europe, France, Belgium, and Holland have been among those who have rejected the symbolism of Islam. Embracing it will be positively viewed in the Islamic world." (American tolerance hadn't saved it from terror.)

Some Muslims were concerned that the proposal heightened the link in people's minds between Islam and terrorism, which we'd tried so hard to avoid. I certainly paid more attention through those weeks to hints of Islam in the news.

A mosque in New York wasn't in the minds of the Taliban when it found five American men, an American woman, a German woman, and a British woman working for the aid organisation International Assistance Mission in northern Afghanistan. It lined up the eight ophthalmologists in dense forest and shot them dead. "They were Christian missionaries and we killed them all," explained Taliban spokesman Zabihullah Mujahed. "They were carrying Persian-language Bibles, a satellite tracking device, and maps."

Saifullah, an Afghan, said the Westerners thought they were safe because they were doctors. He survived by reciting verses of the Koran, so the killers knew he was Muslim.

News reports of the killing of Melbourne crime patriarch Macchour Chaouk a week later made no mention of his religion. That said, the family complained angrily: "The weak, dirty dogs killed him on Ramadan."

A Lebanese immigrant in 1969, by 1975 Chaouk was charged with assault with a weapon. He and his sons' résumé would go onto include burglary, weapons offences, passport fraud, beating a man causing serious injury, heroin trafficking, assaulting police, and several cases of murder. When a police raid found weapons at Chaouk's home, the family said it needed them for protection. It was quite the family business, although Chaouk told an interviewer they were victims of a police campaign of intimidation.

(Muslims producing and distributing heroin aren't being hypocritical. None of it's headed to Muslims.)

Police immediately suspected rival Lebanese clan the Haddaras, although couldn't link Chaouk's killing with two men gunned down shortly afterwards at a poker-machine venue in Lygon Street. I soon stopped looking for Muslims in the news.

Christian evangelist Terry Jones threatened to burn pages from the Koran if plans for the Muslim centre near the former World Trade Centre, New York weren't scrapped. Muslims and Christians alike condemned him.

Queensland University of Technology lawyer Alexander Stewart was more even-handed. In 2010, wearing a black tee shirt with the words "*I'm an atheist (Thank God)*," he released a twelve-minute film showing him burning pages from the Bible and Koran. He used the pages to roll what looked like cannabis cigarettes.

"I don't think on the face of it that what he's done is an offence," commented Queensland Council for Civil Liberties president Michael Cope, "nor do we think it should be." If we're going to upset Muslims, we better upset Christians, too.

Hartford City Council responded to concerns about the proposed mosque in New York by inviting local imams to perform Islamic invocations at the beginning of council meetings through

September. Council president Jo Winch, an African American, called it "an act of solidarity with our Muslim brothers and sisters."

There was no solidarity with victims of Muslim terrorism. They weren't Winch's brothers and sisters. Our dead don't matter.

"I feel it is very important that, as a council," Winch explained, "we project a culture of inclusiveness in the city of Hartford. Too often it is our differences that divide us. In my opinion, it is our combination of differences that makes us strong."

I doubted that I'd ever heard anyone more expert in the nonsensical slogans of our time than Winch. She didn't explain why a combination of differences should make a city strong. It was something to say.

That Wednesday afternoon I'd read about Winch, driving home from work a little after five thirty, I listened to radio station 2BL. Talking about people with different values, the host and his guest took telephone calls from listeners. One talked of a close friend who'd gone to Japan and tried eating whale meat. Eating whale meat, she said, was "a deal-breaker."

Food matters more to the West than eternity, or at least people's beliefs about them. Nothing as trivial as terrorism or religion affects our opinions of strangers, but we walk away from close friends because they eat whale meat. I wondered if she'd walk away from Japanese for that reason.

The next caller complained about her friend's racist boyfriend. We think Muslims are our brothers and sisters, but not racists. Nothing matters more to us than white people's racism; not even whale meat. No combination of differences makes *us* strong.

Luis Cotto liked Hartford City Council hearing Muslim prayers so close to the ninth anniversary of the 2001 attacks. "I thought that doing this in September or at the next meeting, which happens to be September, makes sense," said the councilman, "and I still do."

Many objections weren't so much about Islam as about religion generally. "*Where is the separation between church and state?*" asked one reader of the *NBC Connecticut* website.

The West equates Muslim prayers to Christian ones. We no longer pray.

Winch considered an interfaith prayer before the Monday night meeting two days after the anniversary. "There might be twenty different faiths there on that day because… we have to understand we live in a multicultural city and there are one hundred and twenty-five thousand residents here, so we don't want to have anyone be offended."

Heaven forbid somebody's religion not be included. Council ultimately revoked the whole prayer idea.

Imam Kashif Abdul-Karim complained that the council no longer wanted him leading Muslim prayers. "We feel as though it would be a step backwards because it would be labelling me as part of the problem that took place on nine/eleven, and we had nothing to do with that." (He distanced himself from Islamic terrorism no less than we did.) "It's basically just disrespecting the whole Muslim community by lumping us together with twelve people out of one point five billion people around the world." (Nineteen Muslim terrorists carried out the attacks. They'd become twelve.)

The council held a moment of silence at the beginning of its September meetings. "That way," said Winch, "we are not disrespecting anyone."

We'd removed religion altogether. Meanwhile, unconcerned about offending anyone, Abdul-Karim stood outside Hartford city hall while the Monday night meeting began, praying in English and Arabic.

Immigrants assert their cultures. We're unwilling to assert ours.

17. DEFENDING MULTICULTURALISM

The West doesn't defend our countries, cultures, or races. We defend multiculturalism.

Baghdad-born Taimur Abdulwahab al-Abdaly became a Swedish citizen in 1992, growing up in the town of Tranas, two hundred kilometres from Stockholm. Graduating with a sports therapy degree from the University of Bedfordshire, he cut a dashing figure in a suit and jacket. He married another Swedish citizen, Mona Thwany, the child of an Iraqi man and Romanian woman, who managed a home beauty company. With their three children, they must've seemed our very model of a multicultural family.

Abdulwahab attended Friday prayers at the Islamic Centre in Luton, but wasn't among the Muslims picketing a homecoming parade for British soldiers returning from Iraq to Luton, holding up signs accusing the soldiers of being "*butchers*" and "*baby-killers.*" Nevertheless, they named their son born in 2010 Osama in honour of Osama bin Laden. Also that year, Abdulwahab advertised on the *Muslima* website for a second wife.

In October 2010, security police said the terrorism threat in Sweden remained low compared to that in other European countries. It was a matter of comparison, but police felt no attack was imminent.

In November, Abdulwahab returned to Tranas to visit relatives. On the second Saturday of December, the day before his twenty-ninth birthday, he exploded a car among Christmas shoppers near Drottninggatan in Stockholm, injuring two Swedes. Twelve minutes later and three hundred metres away, a second bomb malfunctioned, killing only him.

Abdulwahab left a message explaining that the bombs were his response to Swedish artist Lars Vilk drawing the prophet Mohammed as a dog, three years earlier. An American citizen calling herself "Jihad Jane" had been charged with plotting to kill

Vilk in March. In May, arsonists tried to set fire to Vilk's house.

Abdulwahab's last message asked his wife to kiss their children on his behalf. "*Tell them Daddy loves them.*" Muslim terrorists are often good family men. We aren't their families.

His bombs were also a response to Swedish soldiers fighting in Afghanistan. "*Now your children, daughters and sisters shall die like our brothers and sisters and children are dying,*" he wrote in an earlier mail message to a Swedish news agency. Swedish citizenship hadn't made Swedes his brothers and sisters, while Islam made Afghans his brothers and sisters. "*Now the Islamic state has been created. We now exist here in Europe and in Sweden. We are a reality… Our actions will speak for themselves.*"

Prime Minister Fredrik Reinfeldt wasn't deterred. "We cherish this society," he said, as if Swedes and immigrants formed a society. "This society is worth defending."

Whatever he cherished wasn't Swedish. Only multiculturalism matters.

Never did the jingoism of our past patriotism rival the jingoism of our postmodern multiculturalism. "*We are the most successful multicultural society in the world,*" Prime Minister Malcolm Turnbull typed into his Facebook computer page in 2015, after an Iranian declaring "*Allahu Akbar!*" murdered a Chinese police accountant outside Parramatta police headquarters. (Other multicultural societies can't be much good.)

We claim success with our multiculturalism, without explaining what makes us successful. "*We live in one of the most successful multicultural and multifaith societies in the world…,*" wrote Victoria Police chief commissioner Ken Lay in 2014. A day earlier, New South Wales and Queensland police raids detained fifteen Muslims suspected of planning to behead strangers.

"But in being vigilant – as we must be – we should not forget the very thing that makes our society so special," continued Lay. "*Please don't let these raids and the revised public-alert level prejudice your view of multiculturalism because of a minority wanting to do harm…. Victoria Police and the broader Victorian community welcome people of all faiths, all backgrounds and all ethnicities. It's why we are a wonderful community and why it is universally acknowledged that our ability to welcome people from the four corners of the globe has been one of our great political and social achievements.*"

The *Age* newspaper introduced Lay's letter with the caption: "*Now, more than ever, we must embrace our multicultural, multifaith environment*." Three days later in Endeavour Hills, Melbourne, eighteen-year-old Numan Haider stabbed two policemen after one tried to shake his hand. Police shot him dead. The newspaper omitted to mention that Haider brandished an Islamic State flag.

Multiculturalism succeeds, because we say it succeeds. A million immigrants could storm the streets of Europe beheading people, for which we'd change the colours on our computer pages in sympathies for the victims (as we did after the Muslim attacks on Paris in November 2015), but we'd still declare multiculturalism a success.

Our strategy for eliminating Islamic terrorism is to continue welcoming more Muslims, defending them from discrimination, and giving them more money and services. It hasn't worked so far.

"While much good work has been done in Australia over many decades, we must continue to work to eliminate all forms of racial discrimination," immigration minister Chris Bowen (an atheist) told the Sydney Institute, the third Wednesday in February 2011. Australia formed yet another advisory body, the Multicultural Advisory Council. "The new body will act as a champion for multiculturalism in the community, will advise the government on multicultural affairs and will help ensure Australian government services respond to the needs of migrant and refugee communities."

Bowen's speech was titled 'What makes multiculturalism great is mutual respect,' steeped in fervent adoration. "I've seen people, wearing the national dress of their homeland, clasping an Australian flag and welling up with tears as they promise to uphold and obey Australian values and laws." (I wonder if that was true.) "They serve as a reminder of what I term 'the genius of Australian multiculturalism'."

Only the West equates freedom and equality with multiculturalism, as if the rest of the world isn't free or equal and we weren't before immigrants came. "If Australia is to be free and equal," declared Bowen, "then it will be multicultural; but if it is to be multicultural it must remain free and equal." It was nonsense.

To his credit, Bowen proceeded to explore the meaning of multiculturalism as few do (although not the meaning of genius). "To some, multiculturalism is simply a diverse population, and a non-discriminatory immigration policy. These are the foundations of Australian multiculturalism, but it consists of much more.

"Firstly, our multiculturalism is underpinned by respect for traditional Australian values. Those who arrive in Australia are invited to continue to celebrate their cultures within a broader culture of freedom but, more importantly, with respect. However, if there is any inconsistency between these values and individual freedom and the rule of law, then these Australian values win out. They must."

That was in spite of multiculturalism advocates like Peter Chambers and Tory Shepherd insisting there were no Australian values, not worthwhile ones anyway. If there'd been Australian values, they were racist.

"This is related to the second element of the genius of Australian multiculturalism," Bowen continued. "Ours is citizenship based; to enjoy the full benefits of Australian society, it is necessary to take a pledge of commitment."

Yet of thirty-six Muslims involved in sixteen Australian terrorism cases studied by Sam Mullins up to 2012, all but two were Australian citizens. Most had lived here for more than ten years with "quite unremarkable backgrounds" before undertaking terrorist activity. Like elsewhere around the West, terrorists are increasingly locally born.

"The third element of the genius of Australian multiculturalism is political bipartisanship," continued Bowen, "particularly at its creation." That was to say, no major political party had questioned it.

Multiculturalism is individualism. "Multiculturalism is about inviting every individual member of society to be everything they can be and supporting each new arrival in overcoming whatever obstacles they face as they adjust to a new country and society and allowing them to flourish as individuals," insisted Bowen. "It is a matter of liberalism. A truly robust liberal society is a multicultural society."

Yet classic liberalism has evaporated under the controls, lies, and censorship of multiculturalism. Freedoms are fewer.

Our predecessors knew our freedoms did not depend upon us giving them to other races. They depended on us not giving some of them. Countries outside the West know their freedoms depend on not giving them to other races, and sometimes to their own.

Britain responded to the 2001 terrorist attacks on America not with constraints upon Muslims, but with laws protecting them from vilification. By 2009, she had thirty-five acts of parliament, fifty-two statutory instruments, thirteen codes of practice, three codes of guidance, and sixteen European Union directives against discrimination.

People who hate harm only themselves, provided they don't hit, rape, or kill others. The emotion grinds away from within. Conversely, people who hit, rape, or kill harm other people, whether or not they happen to hate them. In the West's Age of Ideology, the reasons people slit people's throats matter more than our frail throats being slit.

The Association of Chief Police Officers and the Crown Prosecution Service agreed a definition of a hate crime as a *"criminal offence which is perceived by the victim or any other person, to be motivated by hostility or prejudice based on a person's race or perceived race; religion or perceived religion...."*

The offence doesn't have to be hostile. It merely has to be perceived by another person to have been hostile.

We make only some feelings illegal. Hating rich people or poor people is fine, hating other races or religions isn't. White people unfazed about robbery, rape, and murder become fiery advocates for law and order when someone from another race or religion feels offended.

Actions don't need to be otherwise illegal for perceived prejudice to be a crime. Ben and Sharon Vogelenzang were Christians in Liverpool, England, who had a strongly worded discussion with a Muslim guest at their hotel about the relative merits of their respective religions. No one was hurt, no property damaged, but it led to the Vogelenzangs being prosecuted for a religiously aggravated hate crime.

Although they were ultimately acquitted, the prosecution was a marked contrast with a Muslim man who sprayed the words *"Islam will dominate the world – Osama is on his way"* and *"Kill Gordon Brown"* on a war memorial in Burton-Upon-Trent. (Gordon Brown was British prime minister.) The Muslim was prosecuted for criminal damage but not a hate crime. The Crown Prosecution Service believed the British war memorial "did not attach to any particular racial or religious group."

The dead the memorial honoured were our forebears, but we no longer attach ourselves to them. We've lost all track of our war dead being of our race.

The Muslim hadn't. He defaced the memorial because it honoured our race: us.

Civitas, the Institute for the Study of Civil Society, issued a 2010 report titled *A New Inquisition: religious persecution in Britain today*. The foreword said "*prosecutors and police are unfairly singling out alleged crimes by white Christians, while ignoring other similar offences by minority groups.*"

The Crown Prosecution Service provided tens of thousands of pounds funding the National Black Crown Prosecution Association, whose "*main objective is to advance the careers of ethnic minorities within the CPS but it also takes an interest in the impact of CPS decisions on members of ethnic minorities.*" Civitas cited a newspaper report that "*ethnic minorities were being given jobs within the CPS that they could not do.*"

Employing white people because we could do jobs would be white privilege. Not employing other races because they couldn't those jobs would be institutional racism.

Merely taunting another race or religion is illegal. New York police investigated as a hate crime the discovery of three uncooked packages of bacon in a Staten Island park where Muslims were celebrating the end of Ramadan, 2012.

Englishman Kevin Crehan attacked the Jamia Mosque in Bristol not with guns and bombs, but bacon. He tied it to the mosque's door handles. Sentencing him to nine months in gaol in 2016, Judge Julian Lambert called the incident, in which Crehan also abused a Muslim and tied a St George's flag to the fence, an "attack on England." It wasn't.

New South Wales police were accused of religious insensitivity for raiding a suspected criminal's home during Ramadan, 2009. Apparently, police should've suspended operations involving Muslims that month.

What newspapers didn't report at the time, so far as I noticed, was the ensuing riot by a hundred and fifty Muslim youths in Auburn. The riot became newsworthy when police (having improved their religious sensitivity) blamed it not on Muslims but on the social networking website Facebook, which Muslims used to tell each other that "*non-believers*" were raiding a "*brother's home.*"

The Muslims refused to respect police because police weren't Muslim. Police were Kaffirs.

Respect for courts of law commands that people stand when speaking or being addressed by a judge. Milad Bin Ahmad-Shah al-

Ahmadzai said Islam prevented him standing before Judge Ian McClintock in the District Court, Sydney, the penultimate Friday in May 2014.

Islam hadn't prevented him from threatening the life of an Australian intelligence officer. "I'm gonna crack your neck," al-Ahmadzai told the officer. "Come near my family again, I'm gonna slit your throat, pig."

Nor had Islam prevented him ramming a car into an automatic teller machine in 2011 to rob it, for which he was sentenced to five and a half years gaol. Nor had Islam kept him from attempting to murder a man at Rydalmere in May 2013. He'd been under surveillance by the Joint Counter Terrorism Team since December 2009.

Instead of confronting reality, we lose ourselves in vacuous slogans. "Our ethos is 'One community, proudly diverse'," declared chief executive Peter Brown, explaining why Moreland City Council allowed Hizb ut-Tahrir, the Party of Islamic Liberation, to hire Brunswick Town Hall for a conference in 2010. "This decision is based on our strong belief in political and religious freedom, but council will remain vigilant and ensure that our city's facilities are not used to incite violence, racism, sexism, or religious intolerance."

Council's vigilance seemed only to be directed at white people. Hizb ut-Tahrir advocated a global Islamic caliphate, believing armed conflict was a legitimate response to defend the caliphate from the West. It said insurgents fighting against Australian and allied troops in Iraq had a "universal right and religious duty."

Believing that "democracy is a bankrupt and irrational idea," a recent Hizb ut-Tahrir gathering in Sydney urged Muslims to shun democracy altogether. Only Allah, not people, can make laws, so that democracy is inherently incompatible with Islam. It believed that "all indicators are pointing to the decline and inevitable collapse of Western ideology."

Hizb ut-Tahrir was right about Western ideology. We persist with ideology regardless.

With the comfort of our convictions that immigrants are like the rest of us, joined with us in our mythical multicultural society, we identify them accordingly. 'Australian's passport seized in Jordan,' headed a 2011 news report, referring to Ismail al-Wahwah. Jordanian authorities weren't as relaxed as Moreland City Council would've been about his membership of Hizb ut-Tahrir.

Nothing deters us from defending diversity in our multicultural wonderland. "The corrupt and illegitimate ruling systems," said Australian spokesman for Hizb ut-Tahrir, Uthman Badar, in 2011, "which represent neither Islam nor Muslims, need to be uprooted entirely and replaced with the system of Islam which safeguards the rights and dignity of all citizens."

In 2013, Hizb ut-Tahrir called on Australia to become an Islamic state ruled by Islamic law and for a boycott of Anzac Day. "There is a ridiculous amount of surveillance by ASIO and tapping of phones," complained Badar, accusing the Australian Security and Intelligence Organisation of demonising Muslims. "You are further alienating these people."

Multiculturalism is not liberalism. Racial and religious diversity requires increased surveillance and other security: a role for the state tantamount to dictatorship. A world without borders is a world of conflict and turmoil, until martial law takes control.

18. WARTIME PROPAGANDA

When I was at school, geography was the study of the earth's landforms and waterways. Not anymore. My eldest son's year-ten geography class learnt about human rights, but not his. For his assignment he chose Somalia, after seeing the 2001 film *Black Hawk Down*. The film began with a quote from the ancient Greek philosopher Plato. "*Only the dead have seen an end to war.*"

A draft version of the script began with a quote from English poet T.S. Eliot. "*All our ignorance brings us closer to death.*"

With the threat of war growing, the 1937 British film *O.H.M.S.* tried to stir pacifist Britain towards militarism by portraying British Army life as adventurous. Allied propaganda during the Second World War, such as the 1942 film *The Day Will Dawn*, encouraged Britons to fight Germans. Western propaganda now encourages us *not* to fight Muslims.

My second daughter was surprised to see one of the names ascribed to a fictional character in her year eight of school, 2012: Adolf. Rest assured, Adolf was a bad boy, "*determined to make life as difficult as possible for all those around him… He's failed all subjects this year and been suspended three times. If Adolf's performance does not improve next term, I'll have no choice but to recommend his expulsion.*"

In contrast were the three other fictional characters in unit 17, question 2 of her apostrophes revision exercise. Sarah and Georgina were joys to teach and excellent students, but the real standout among the four in academic performance and good character was Omar. "*It's a pleasure to have him in my class!*" Arabs never looked so good.

In Western eyes, Islam's failings blemish all religion. Its successes are its alone.

Among them were the Muslim invasions of Europe, such as the Moors occupying what became Spain and Portugal for almost eight hundred years, before the Spanish evicted the last of them in 1616. Turkish invasions of Europe reached the gates of Vienna in 1529 and 1683. Among the many countries occupied by the Turks was

Bulgaria, which didn't regain her independence until 1878. After five hundred years, the Balkan League evicted the last of the Turks from the Balkans in 1912.

The multiculturalist West is not so xenophobic. We'd have hugged the Moors and Turks. We'd have bombed the Spaniards and Balkan League.

Foreigners have ceased entering Europe by invasion. Since World War II, they've come through our open arms.

We only mention past invasions to appreciate their intervention. The British Broadcasting Corporation website said the television documentary *An Islamic Invasion of Europe*, broadcast in 2007, "*looks back to a golden age when European civilisation was enriched by Islamic learning.*" The programme host "*travels across medieval Muslim Europe to reveal the vibrant civilisation that Muslims brought to the West. This evocative film brings to life a time when emirs and caliphs dominated Spain and Sicily and Islamic scholarship swept into the major cities of Europe. His journey reveals the debt owed to Islam for its vital contribution to the European Renaissance.*"

It was a lie, while Christianity's role leading the Renaissance no longer warrants a mention. No other race on earth speaks so fondly of being invaded as we now do.

In a similar vein, former Australian diplomat Tony Kevin described the last Moor stronghold in Spain, Grenada, as a sort of multicultural nirvana before the intolerant Spaniards defeated the emirate in 1492. That might seem long ago, but 1492 was also the year Christopher Columbus arrived in the Americas. White Americans now regard themselves as occupiers of other people's land.

Half-Jewish Kevin admitted an affinity for the Jews also expelled from Spain in 1492. Funnily enough, he was addressing St Ives Baptist Church that third Sunday in May 2012 about his book *Walking the Camino*, concerning Catholic pilgrimages in Spain.

While we consider Europe's empires across the world to have been bad invasions, we consider Moorish and Turkish invasions of Europe good invasions. The messages are clear: we owe them. The more that come, the more they enrich us. Subjugation and deaths aren't devastating when inflicted upon us.

Other races agree. In 2010, Melbourne University's Centre for Excellence in Islamic Studies published a guide to teaching Islam in schools. It listed al-Qaeda among the "*famous names*" and terrorism among the several *"constant reminders of this distrust"* between the West and Islam, making terrorism as much our fault as theirs. It blamed high Muslim unemployment not on Muslims, but on the *"underlying discrimination and prejudice towards non-Europeans in Australia."*

We're never more trusting than we are of advertisements. In 2011, Australian Muslims and others funded the 'My Peace' television commercials promoting what they said were Islamic values. Lawyer Mariam Veiszadeh called it a response to the *"lies, fabrications and distortions attributed to our faith... not only... from so-called adherents of Islam who have twisted its teachings to justify their criminal acts, but also from media organisations and policy makers who are content to spread misrepresentations about Islam and Muslims, to serve their own interests."*

I'm not sure what misrepresentations Veiszadeh meant. Never did I read a newspaper gush forth about a church as the *Sydney Morning Herald* newspaper gushed forth about the Auburn Gallipoli mosque and its tenth annual open day. 'Mosque opens its doors,' declared the headline, 'and visitors open their minds.'

With our devotion to multiculturalism guiding us, we believe we open our minds when we believe good things about immigrants. We believe we close our minds when we pay heed to the bad things about immigrants.

The open days had been the mosque's response to the 2001 terrorist attacks in America, marketing Islam. Rioting, crime, and terrorism could all be forgotten over what journalist Damien Murphy called *"a lavish smorgasbord"* lunch. Cultural understanding meant judging Muslims by their food instead of anything else, although smorgasbords originated in Sweden. (Increasingly, so are Muslims.)

A few months later, the same newspaper's article about Eid ul-Adha, a four-day celebration coinciding with the end of the Muslim pilgrimage to Mecca, was always going to be about Muslims. Titled 'A time to celebrate – and enjoy peace and harmony,' it was a sweet, pretty image in words and photograph.

Much, much briefer was the previous day's article about Muslims. Those Muslims murdered a hundred and fifty people in north-eastern Nigeria.

During Iraq's war with Iran during the 1980s, Iraqi film-makers broadcast stories from history of Arab victories against Persians. We on the other hand, with our non-war against Muslims, trawl through history to find wrongful acts by Christians. Unable to find them, we concoct them.

The 2009 Spanish film *Agora* claimed that fourth-century Christian zealots suppressed knowledge and oppressed people in the Roman city of Alexandria, Egypt, although there is no evidence that any of the wrongful acts by Christians depicted in the film actually occurred. Directed and co-written by homosexual Alejandro Amenabar and starring a Jewess, Rachel Weisz, the film created a fictional Christian past seventeen hundred years earlier. It made Christians the threat.

Insisting all cultures are equal, we're determined to avoid any morsel of moral superiority above Muslims. Our enemy is white racism.

The greatest threat to the fictional president Josiah Bartlet in the American television series *The West Wing* wasn't Muslim terrorism but white racists, when Bartlet's daughter was involved with a black man. The episode 'Isaac and Ishmael,' written after the 2001 attacks, equated Islam with Christianity and Muslim terror with the Ku Klux Klan.

Whatever stories we tell, the villains aren't Muslims. They're Christians.

In the 2007 American screenplay *Dubai*, the 2001 terrorist attacks were the inspiration for the protagonist to become a Central Intelligence Agency operative. When the screenplay became the 2013 film *Jack Ryan: Shadow Recruit*, all mention of Muslims had gone, bar one reference to the Mujahedeen in Afghanistan. Instead, the villains had become Russian nationalists, several of whom lived in America and at least one of which was an American citizen.

The day before the tenth anniversary of the Muslim terrorist attacks on London of the seventh of July 2005, the *Australian Broadcasting Corporation News* channel 24 six o'clock evening bulletin described the terrorists only as British. The only person interviewed about her frightening experiences that day was South Asian. Any viewer whose only knowledge of the attacks was that report would assume four Englishmen murdered fifty-two immigrants.

Channel 99 (Go!) marked the tenth anniversary by showing, at eight thirty that evening, the 2005 American and German film *V for Vendetta*. (I'd already seen it.) Based upon a graphic novel published during the 1980s, the film portrayed a terrorist heroically leading a British revolution against a ruthless Conservative Party dictatorship. (In 2005, the Conservative Party had been out of power in Britain for almost a decade. This was before Conservative Party governments ceased being a problem.) In the world of the film, the writers added intolerance of Islam to the crimes of a Christian regime.

In an education system that prohibits celebration of Christianity for the offence that it causes, my eldest son's English class watched *V for Vendetta*, the third Tuesday in February of his penultimate year in high school, 2012. It was part of a study into power and control, implicitly by Christians (rather than by our new Western education systems).

Moments of humour laced the film. Ideology doused it. The hero of the story was V: a masked terrorist attacking Christian and conservative Britons.

Behind a wine rack in the home of the charming and sophisticated middle-aged Gordon Deitrich was a secret room, hiding artistic treasures from the tyrannical British government. Particularly special was a book sealed in a glass case: a fourteenth century copy of the Koran. He introduced it to a young woman, Evey, saying he was not Musim but still founds its images beautiful and poetry moving. If the Biblical Eve was the first woman, then Evey was the first of a new kind of European: one admiring Islam.

The irony of the room being behind a wine rack given Muslim attitudes to alcohol seemed as lost on Deitrich as it was on everyone else. Alcohol paled aside Deitrich being homosexual, as was the actor playing him, Stephen Fry. Fry was also a Jew.

Evey quotes her father, a writer, to say that artists use lies to tell the truth, while politicians use lies to conceal the truth. They were words of ideology, by which lies are the truth and the truth is a lie. Heroes and villains are liars, although heroes claim the mantle of truth behind theirs. We're left only with lies. Communist relativism had become Western relativism.

No characters in the film were obviously Muslim or adherents to any other religion, except Christianity. The bishop was a paedophile, whose church procured young women for him to molest. This wasn't a world where paedophiles were homosexual.

No Christian country on earth punishes people for possessing a Koran but, in the film, Deitrich is executed for doing so. In the real world, the year after the film's release, Victorian county hospitals removed Bibles from its rooms for fear of offending non-Christians.

In the film, the British government masterminded plagues that killed more than eighty thousand people. Only Christians and conservatives could we portray as so comprehensively evil: as evil at all.

V killed civilians for what the film-makers considered a much-greater good. The film's happy ending was the Conservative Party leader dead, multiracial crowds overrunning the police and army, and a bomb destroying the Houses of Parliament.

It all came together most succinctly with two strangely inhuman voices, much like the voices in lifts, over the closing credits of the film. A male voice quoted black American Malcolm X exhorting violence against white Americans: "Concerning non-violence, it is criminal to teach man not to defend himself when he is the constant victim of brutal attacks." We no longer contemplate white people defending ourselves from attacks.

A female voice, of sorts, promoted humanism, without sex or race but with roles chosen or earned. It could have been Soviet communism but was Western individualism, both of them multiculturalism, grounded in ideology.

Humanism dehumanises. We can have all the choices we want (except Christianity and conservatism), subject to our nationless, raceless, and cultureless human authorities deciding what we've earned. Our human authorities organise us not by human biology and relationship, but by whatever political or economic objective they dictate. They've proven willing to let us die, even kill us.

Anti-Christian revolutionaries in the film wore masks associated with English traitor Guy Fawkes, a convert to Roman Catholicism. Muslim Egyptians climbing the walls of the American embassy in Cairo on Tuesday, the eleventh day of September 2012, tearing apart an American flag and replacing it with a black al-Qaeda flag, wore the same masks.

It is easy to dismiss *V for Vendetta* as a propaganda piece for militant Marxism and Islam against their common enemy, the Christian West, but at least one reviewer realised the Islam portrayed was a secular one. Poetry mattered, not religion. It's our vision for a multicultural world without religion, where Islam is a revered culture without Allah: an atheistic, godless Islam, as only the West imagines.

There's little wonder Muslims attack us with such a vision in place, but we have to redefine Islam. Muslims would be far less tolerant than Christians and Jews of the writers of the film, brothers Larry and Andy Wachowski. Larry wore women's clothes, took female hormones, and liked to be called Lana.

By 2016, Andy was doing the same. He liked to be called Lilly.

19. CHRISTIANS

The West refuses to fear other races and cultures. We fear only white people and cultures.

In 2019, *The Guardian* newspaper article 'Rise in UK use of far-right online forums as anti-Muslim hate increases' made much of the supposed threat from white people, although tucked into the eighth paragraph was a salient point: "*However, MI5 said the volume of rightwing cases was 'absolutely dwarfed by the number of Islamist cases'.*" I was somewhat surprised that the editor let that line through to publication.

The exoneration of bad Muslims from being real Muslims isn't one we extend to bad Christians. Only good Christians can renounce their religion: their Christian identity.

Religion is never more relevant than when a criminal is Christian. 'Exclusive Brethren member on rape charge,' headed Nick Clark's 2009 article in the *Mercury* newspaper.

Nor did the 2011 headline in the *Age* newspaper shy away from identifying Craig John Coleman's religion: 'Porn-addict Christian father admits abusing 3-year-old.' He was "*a member of a western suburbs Pentecostal congregation.*"

Robyn Ironside's 2010 article in the *Courier-Mail* newspaper was the same. 'Catholic teacher Gerard Byrnes jailed for 10 years for raping, molesting 13 students.'

Child abuse doesn't taint teachers, politicians, or anyone else as it taints clergymen. They're treated as conspirators for failing to understand the torment the abuse caused, at a time only the victims understood. Naïvety is no excuse.

We impose upon white people collective culpabilities for crime and terror we don't impose upon others. In their 2010 article for the *Health Sociology Review* journal, 'Suicide by mass murder: Masculinity, aggrieved entitlement, and rampage school shootings,' Jewish sociologists Rachel Kalish and Michael Kimmel "*proposed a mechanism that might well explain why white males are routinely going crazy and killing people,*" in the words of commentator William Hamby writing for the *Atlanta Atheism Examiner* in 2012. "*Most likely not coincidental is the fact that since 1982, one very specific type of mass shootings has been almost entirely perpetrated by white males.*"

Those words were simply untrue, and not only because the deadliest school massacre was committed by a Korean, Seung-Hui Cho, at the Virginia Polytechnic Institute and State University in 2007. Even if a disproportionately high number of mass school shootings have been perpetrated by white males, it isn't routine. Disproportionately high numbers of other crimes, including murder, by other races haven't led us to contemplate analyses about them.

Hamby blamed the school shootings on white males supposedly resenting their loss of power, which in the West's pursuit of equality (more fanatical than any religion) Hamby thought was a good thing. Hamby was a white male, who presumably did not resent his loss of power. He was also a human rights advocate.

He became specific. "*Speaking of strongly Conservative Christian areas… I think it's important to at least entertain the idea that strongly conservative religious communities which indoctrinate young white men into male superiority are breeding grounds for these kinds of criminals.*"

None of the school shooters held Christian faith, but Hamby considered the possibility that religious communities around them fostered their violence. It's the approach that blames Christian Europe for the Holocaust, in spite of the Nazi leadership having no Christian faith.

We don't entertain that idea about other races or religions. Nor do we entertain it about opponents of religion.

News services rushed to say Chris Harper-Mercer had a British father, after he murdered nine students at the Umpqua Community College in Roseburg, Oregon the first day of October 2015. *Cable News Network* correspondent Pamela Brown reported the murderer's apparent writings that "rambled about his hatred towards black men." Few reports mentioned that his mother was black.

Stacy Boylen, whose daughter was wounded, said the gunman asked "people one by one what their religion was. 'Are you a Christian?' he would ask them, 'and if you're a Christian stand up,' and they would stand up and he said, 'Good, because you're a Christian, you are going to see God in just about one second,' and then he shot and killed them."

"The shooter was lining people up and asking if they were christian," wrote bodhilooney on the Twitter website. Her grandmother was at the college during the carnage. *"If they said yes, then they were shot in the head. If they said no, or didn't answer, they were shot in the legs."*

The gunman was a member of a website group that *"doesn't like organised religion."* The campus had decided the previous year not to arm security guards.

In April 2009, the Department of Homeland Security issued a report prepared by the Office of Intelligence and Analysis titled *Right Wing Extremism: Current Economic and Political Climate Fuelling Resurgence in Radicalisation and Recruitment*. Labelled as right-wing extremists were white Americans concerned about illegal immigration, abortion, firearms control, and the expansion of federal powers.

There was no evidence they were planning acts of violence, but the report warned that *"right-wing extremists capitalized on the election of the first African American president, and are focusing their efforts to recruit new members, mobilize existing supporters and broaden their scope and appeal through propaganda, but they have not yet turned to attack planning."* War veterans were particular targets for recruitment because their *"combat skills and experience"* encouraged *"violent capabilities."*

Such commentary was unthinkable about other races. Department secretary Janet Napolitano said of the report, "it rang true with me, this has happened in the past."

Forty-two million military veterans had risked their lives for America's sake, many of them incurring injuries. The government's concern was premised upon the actions of one, and that was fourteen years earlier. On the nineteenth day of April 1995, Timothy McVeigh set the bomb that destroyed the Alfred P. Murrah government building in Oklahoma City, killing a hundred and sixty-eight people. McVeigh was executed.

Napolitano apologised for the offence caused veterans, while reminding them that McVeigh "was a vet." We had no caveat for the majority of peace-loving veterans, or a disclaimer that McVeigh wasn't a real veteran. The American Army didn't train McVeigh in bomb making. He was a gunner, who'd learnt to make bombs after leaving the military.

McVeigh's conspirator Terry Nichols, who was imprisoned for life, was an American Army veteran, although seems not to have influenced the 2009 report. Other conspirators Michael and Lori

Fortier gave evidence for the prosecution, but they weren't veterans. They were friends of McVeigh.

The son of divorced parents, McVeigh was agnostic. He said science was his religion.

McVeigh set the bomb to explode exactly two years after agents from the Department of Alcohol, Tobacco, and Firearms ended the fifty-one day siege of the Branch Davidian cult in Waco, Texas because cult members had allegedly breached firearm laws. (Hearing there were any firearms laws in Texas surprised me.) Instead of waiting, the agents killed seventy-six cult members, including children. Along with the Ruby Ridge siege in Idaho in 1992, in which three people died, the deaths convinced McVeigh that the American government was at war with her people. He believed, wrongly, that the agents at Waco had been based in the Alfred P. Murrah building.

The Department of Homeland Security warning fourteen years later was based upon McVeigh being white and a veteran. It made no warning about agnostics or the children of divorcees.

We have no trouble linking political opinion to crime and terrorism. Commentators assumed Jared Lee Loughner was a conservative Christian when, on the second Saturday of January 2011, he killed six people and wounded eighteen others including Democrat congresswomen Gabrielle Giffords, a Jewess, in Tucson. Pima County sheriff Clarence Dupnik condemned "the vitriol that comes out of certain mouths about tearing down the government," which could've meant the political discourse that had become the norm in America for years. With Democrats in power, he had his mind on Republicans.

The *Cable News Network* was among many news services to discuss the likelihood the killer was inspired to violence by former Alaska governor Sarah Palin and other conservative Christian Republicans. "Even though, as you point out," Jessica Yellin told Wolf Blitzer, "this suspect is not co-operating with investigators, so we don't know the motive. President Obama also delivered that message, saying it's partly the political rhetoric that led to this… As you might recall, back in March of last year, when the healthcare vote was coming to the floor of the House and this was all heating up, Palin tweeted out a message on Twitter saying 'common sense conservatives, don't retreat – instead reload,' and she referred folks to her Facebook page. On that Facebook page was a list of

Democratic members she was putting in cross hairs, and Gabrielle Giffords was one of those in the cross hairs."

In fact, Loughner was an atheist and nihilist. Registered not as a Republican but an independent, he'd been far more antagonist to former president George W. Bush, a conservative Christian Republican, than to most Democrats. His motives for the shooting were towards Giffords personally. He had no interest in healthcare, certainly not in Tucson that day.

In 2011, as part of the ten-million-dollar 'See Something, Say Something' programme, the Department of Homeland Security published a ten-minute film encouraging Americans to report suspicious activity. It told viewers not to pay attention to a person's race in deciding whether a person was a terrorist, but went onto show almost entirely white actors as suspected terrorists. The patriotic Americans reporting them were almost entirely black, Asian, or Arab.

The department's internal lists of people most likely to be terrorists were predominantly white conservatives, including gun owners, supporters of libertarian senator Ron Paul, and enthusiasts for gold bullion. As I read about them, I tried to think of any terrorist attack by those people. There'd been no terrorist act by white people since the Oklahoma City bombing, sixteen years earlier.

When Treynor High School in Iowa planned a terror drill in 2011, the pretend-terrorists shooting dozens of people weren't Muslims. In the fictitious scenario, they were white supremacists concerned about illegal immigration. "This is purely the backdrop and the setup, if you will, to help create a perception of reality for the responders," explained Doug Reed, who planned the exercise.

It was a curious sense of reality: imagining an influx of illegal immigrants to Treynor, where less than one percent of the seven hundred and thirty-five public school students were racial minorities. Treynor Community Schools superintendent Kevin Elwood wasn't aware of local racial tensions or white supremacists.

"We are trying to get this stopped, because all it is doing is building up prejudices by calling people white supremacists and stuff like that," said Craig Halverson, national director of the Minuteman Patriots opposing illegal immigration. "We are mad at the government for ignoring illegal immigration, but nobody is going to run out there and start killing people in Iowa or anything like that."

The drill was cancelled, but not because of white people's sensitivities. An anonymous caller threatened a real shooting.

That call may have been a hoax. What gutted me that year happened in Norway on the twenty-second of July. A blond-haired blue-eyed Norwegian, Anders Breivik, murdered seventy-seven people, almost all of them fellow Norwegians. We were at war with ourselves, had been for a while, and left me wondering what we'd become.

The killings were notable for a terrorist's race, colour, and religion suddenly being newsworthy, and for the extensive coverage of victims. The *Sydney Morning Herald* newspaper displayed their names, faces, and lives, as it hadn't from Muslim terrorism.

We had a palpable enthusiasm for white people being terrorists. Aside from the self-promoting Osama bin Laden, Muslim terrorist's names quickly disappeared. Breivik's name remained at the fore. There were no disclaimers Breivik wasn't a real Christian, although he wasn't part of a church and had no Christian faith. I read of him called a cultural Christian, because he was white and identified with Christianity. We're Christians when we commit terror.

No Muslim terrorist was called a cultural Muslim. None was called a Muslim at all.

I suddenly doubted what I was writing so hard to defend. I never read Muslims doubting their civilisation or civilisations, but we'd not linked Islam to terror.

We didn't talk of Breivik being lost as we talked of Muslim terrorists being lost. There were no pleas to understand him as we try to understand Muslim grievances, no calls to comprehend, no sense we should sit down with him to communicate. Instead, we called him evil and mad, hating him with vengeance we refuse to feel towards Muslim terrorists.

Satirical American website *The People's Cube* understood very well. Parodying our responses to Muslim terrorism, its fictitious news reports included President Barack Obama declaring Christianity a "religion of peace" and praising moderate Christians. The American Board of Education was going to institute a "Christian for a Day" programme in public schools. It was even considering celebrating Christmas.

Muslim terror inspired talk about how horribly we'd supposedly treated Muslims for as long as there have been Muslims (if not longer) and our need to integrate them better. Breivik's terror inspired the same.

Instead of the killing being reason to discuss immigration, it was another reason for silence. "I think it's a very emotional discussion because of what happened in July," said politician Robert Wright, a former head of the Oslo schools board, in November, "and for that reason politicians don't want to enter the discussion at all, because they are afraid."

Non-Nordic peoples amounted to twenty-eight percent of Oslo's population. The previous year, the Bjerke Upper Secondary School in Oslo had suffered an exodus of Norwegian children not wanting to be a minority in the classroom. Trying to keep more from leaving, the school gave Norwegian children their own classes and filled one of three general studies classes with pupils of immigrant parents.

Norwegians departing didn't concern Oslo education commissioner Torge Ødegaard. He pressured the school to integrate classes.

"*Some people blamed the Bible for Breivik's massacre*," wrote journalist Daniel Piotrowski early December, "*others Muslims, others video games and heavy metal. We blamed just one thing: hate.*"

The West assumes terrorists kill from hate because we understand hate. Hating more than we used to hate, we hate prejudice. I've never seen the hatred levelled at people for their race or religion that I've seen levelled at white people wanting to retain their countries or otherwise loyal to their race or religion. We laud other races with all glories, but spit to death anyone among us who breathes a few glories of our own. We damn and despise any self-respecting racism that bravely bares itself among us. No hatred is more vehement than the hatred white people feel for each other.

What we don't understand is love. Psychiatrists Synne Serheim and Torgeir Husby examined Breivik after the massacre. They concluded that he was insane, and that he'd killed "out of love for his people."

In his 2012 essay '*Éloge Littéraire d'Anders Breivik*,' or 'Literary Elegy of Anders Breivik,' French writer Richard Millet blamed Breivik's actions on immigration, which necessitated a defender of Norwegian society acting as he did. "Multiculturalism," he told *France Info* radio on the twenty-seventh day of August, "as it has been imported from the United States, is the worst thing possible for Europe... and creates a mosaic of ghettoes in which the nation no longer exists."

Facing the necessity of war, our forebears across Europe and her colonies sent men like Breivik to fight and die. They fought to save us when necessity demanded harming those threatening us, without the hatred we mete out. If there was feeling, there was love for our races, cultures, and countries. "*Greater love hath no man,*" recorded Victoria's Shrine of Remembrance of those who gave up their lives in the Great War. The words were Christ's, beginning chapter 15, verse 13 of the Gospel of John. "Greater love has no one than this: to lay down one's life for one's friends."

Our forebears wanted peace. The wars they fought for peace, we no longer fight.

We love less than we used to love; we don't really love anything. We don't understand devotion: people valuing a greater good enough to be willing to fight and die. We just die. We talk of the world but value little more than our individual selves, and even that not very much. Breivik's killings were remarkable not because they occurred, but because they'd not occurred sooner and more often.

20. ISLAMIC LAND

Equality is Western ideology. Other races discriminate. Sharia includes the concept of dhimmi, by which Muslim countries allow non-believers limited rights of residence in return for paying punitive rates of taxation.

In 2009, A (H1N1) swine 'flu broke out in Mexico and spread rapidly into America and other countries. Although there'd been no reported cases in Egypt, the Egyptian government rejected World Health Organisation advice and began slaughtering the estimated two hundred and fifty thousand pigs in Egypt. Muslims consider pigs unclean, so their principal owners were Christian garbage collectors, who let the pigs feed from organic waste. The principal buyers of pork were also Christians.

Moroccan writer Tahar Ben Jelloun believed the Egyptian government "clearly acted under pressure from Islamists" when it ordered the killing. Coptic Christians had been in Egypt since before Mohammed was born, but the Muslim Brotherhood opposed rearing pigs "on Islamic land."

When we're not excusing Muslim terror because of our supposed ancient actions, we're excusing them because of our current actions, such as our support since the Second World War for Jewish land. Israel was the Jews' ancient home and the target of several waves of Jewish immigration from Europe and elsewhere since Spain evicted Jews in 1492, but emboldened Arabs through the twentieth century decided the whole Middle East is intrinsically Arab. No Jewish or other enclave warrants a country there being anything but Muslim. Arabs would gleefully expel or obliterate six million Israeli Jews.

Established in 1994, the Palestinian Authority's first law made selling land to Jews a capital offence. Scores of Arab land sellers were soon found dead in Jerusalem, Judea, and Samaria in both judicial and extrajudicial killings. In 2012, the authority sentenced former Palestinian intelligence official Muhammad Abu Shahala to death for selling his home in Hebron to Jews.

Unlike Europeans, Jewish birth rates are highest where they're most under threat, but their rate in Israel remains less than Arab rates. My half-Lebanese old school friend Mark told me in 2006 of a saying among Palestinian Arabs: "Have a baby, and kill an Israeli." It's a demographic war, waged with babies. With enough Muslims in that rare Middle East democracy, Israel will eventually vote itself out of existence.

Commemorating the twentieth anniversary of the National Endowment for Democracy in November 2003, America's President George W. Bush sought to advance a "global democratic revolution." Unwilling to consider race or religion rationally, he rejected the idea that Islam or any other culture could not be democratic. After essentially summarising liberal democracy, he declared: "These vital principles are being applied in the nations of Afghanistan and Iraq."

America and Britain sacrificed thousands of lives and trillions of dollars to make those countries what we think the world can be. They failed.

In 2006, Swiss insurance executive Raymond called Bush "the world's biggest terrorist," with more passion than I'd heard him speak about anything else, even insurance. The judgement Raymond imposed on the American was unlike any he imposed upon Muslims.

Our brief conversation in Bangkok hadn't been about terrorism, but about Bush. Raymond might've been thinking about America's retaliation on Afghanistan immediately after the 2001 attacks, as if there'd have been no war but for Bush's war on terrorism. He was almost certainly thinking about Bush and Britain's Prime Minister Tony Blair leading their coalition of the willing to invade Iraq in March 2003, triumphantly removing Iraq's tyrannical dictator Saddam Hussein.

Hussein had invaded Iran in 1980 and Kuwait in 1990. Threatening more countries in 2003, removing Hussein from power would be another of our so-called humanitarian wars, but people who'd supported the West's war against Christian Serbia in 1999 opposed Blair and Bush's war against Muslim Iraq in 2003.

France and Germany believed (as did the rest of the world) Hussein's bluff that he harboured weapons of mass destruction but, with their large Muslim populations, worked hard against America. They wanted the liberal democracy in Iraq that Bush and

Blair wanted but bought with money not war. Grand naïvety from all sides mars the politics by which we battle each other.

Americans protested Bush and Blair's proposed invasion of Iraq because black Americans were a disproportionately high number of military personnel. They relaxed their objection upon learning blacks were a disproportionately low number of combat personnel. Black Americans at their desks would be safe (although they hadn't been in the Pentagon military headquarters in September 2001). White soldiers could die.

Western Christians were at the forefront of opposing the war. Other critics accused Bush of attacking Iraq to fulfil Biblical prophecy.

At least one expert expected the invasion to be in the Iraqi people's interest. He questioned whether it would be in Britain or America's interest.

Bush and Blair wouldn't have cared about America and Britain's interests. That would be nationalism. Blair seemed to see himself throughout as a latter-day Winston Churchill.

We assume people of other races freed from tyranny will embrace liberal democracy because we have. They do not.

Iraqis embraced democracy only if they thought they'd win. Conditions in Iraq worsened. Civil war replaced tyranny.

Western opponents of the invasion enjoyed the mayhem. The comeuppance we wanted America to feel was more than the comeuppance of the big boy on the block. It was Western comeuppance.

Iraqis angry at American arrogance trying to shore up Iraqi democracy still envied her material wealth. "American go home!" they shouted, according to a radio report in Sydney late in 2006, before adding with black humour reminiscent of Soviet communism, "and take me with you!"

Americans did. The globalism that sends white soldiers to die for other races beckons those other races to come. Western leaders failing to bring liberal democracy to Iraq and Afghanistan presume they can maintain liberal democracy at home while admitting Iraqis and Afghans.

The Iraq War cost many more American and British lives than had the 2001 Muslim attacks on America. Trillions of wasted dollars exacerbated if not created an economic downturn. Bush was deeply unpopular, seeming unsure of what he wanted the

Middle East to be. His Republican Party became disorientated, fractured around issues including immigration and the treatment of terrorists.

Churchill's war against Germany empowered races hostile to Britons. Bush and Blair's war against Hussein empowered Iraqis hostile to Christians.

There'd been more than a million Christians in Iraq before the Iraq War. More than half of them may well have fled after Hussein's removal, without militia to protect them. Muslims beheaded and mutilated a priest in 2006 (despite the payment of a ransom), abducted an archbishop in 2008, and set daisy chains of bombs outside nine churches and fourteen Christian family homes. In October 2010, Muslims killed fifty-eight Christian Chaldeans including two priests in Our Lady of Salvation Church in Baghdad.

The West's rejection of religious difference refuses to find common ground with Christians. Caring about Christians would be discriminatory.

On New Year's Day 2011, twenty-three Coptic Christians were killed and seventy-nine injured when a bomb exploded in the Al-Qiddissin Church in Alexandria, Egypt. Police in France and several other European countries increased security at Coptic churches before the Eastern Orthodox Christmas.

It led also to a rare expression of support for Christians in the Middle East, although President Nicolas Sarkozy might've been posturing to a portion of French public opinion concerned about Islam. (Sarkozy was partly Jewish, abandoned by his father and raised to be Roman Catholic. As interior minister, he'd supported the formation of the *Conseil Français du Culte Musulman*, the French Council of the Muslim Faith.) "We cannot accept and thereby facilitate what looks more and more like a particularly wicked programme of cleansing in the Middle East," he remarked in his annual New Year's address to religious leaders, "religious cleansing."

The *Middle East Online* news service captioned Sarkozy's photograph with the words *"Pot calls the kettle black,"* in spite of France accepting two hundred thousand legal immigrants a year and granting citizenship to a hundred thousand, most of them Muslim. Arabs equated Middle Eastern murders with France recently banning the burqa.

Enforcing its vision of a secular state, France had banned visible religious symbols from government schools in 2004. Nobody cared about banning Christian Crosses, but Muslims demanded their girls wear headscarves. Muslims around the world, who'd cheered France a year or two earlier for opposing the American-led invasion of Iraq, again hated France. (None of the applause we receive from other races lasts beyond the next time we fail to submit to them.) Iraqis kidnapped two French reporters and held them for a hundred and twenty-four days, threatening to kill them if the French ban wasn't reversed.

There's been no immigration to Muslim countries like Muslim and other immigration to the West, only emigration. Through the twentieth century, Christians fell from being twenty percent of the Middle Eastern population to five percent, according to the Vatican. The largest Christian community is in Egypt, but the proportion of Christians fell from twenty percent fifty years earlier to ten percent by 2011.

Much of what became Islamic land had been Christian land. The 1932 census reported fifty-four percent of Lebanese were Christians descended from the Phoenicians, but the 1943 Lebanese Constitution insisted Lebanon be a country with an *"Arab face."* Civil war erupted in 1975, but conflicts that made the West abandon our identities made identities more important in Lebanon. President Bachir Gemayel, a Christian, coined the term dhimmitude in 1982 to describe Muslim majorities subordinating Christian and other minorities.

At the end of the civil war in 1990, the new Constitution called Lebanon *"an Arab country."* The cedars of Lebanon previously Phoenician became Arab.

Lebanon hasn't carried out a national census since 1932 for fear of what it would reveal. The American Central Intelligence Agency World Fact Book in 2011 estimated that Christians numbered forty percent of the country's population. It remained by far the largest percentage of Christians in any Middle Eastern country, but Lebanon had become Muslim.

The West draws no more lessons from the Middle East than from anywhere else. We keep accepting immigrants without distinction between one race and another, one religion or another, trying to make the world anew. We soon forget conflicts to which we're not party, as we soon forget most things.

"After surviving millennia of religious and cultural persecution in its own

cradle," wrote commentator May Akl in the Lebanese newspaper *The Daily Star* in 2010, *"Christianity in the Middle East could face demise at the hands of the Christian West. In fact, political alliances sought by Western states and, most importantly, by the US leverage existential threats against the remaining Christian minorities in the Middle East."*

America's huge payments of aid to Egypt and Pakistan haven't depended upon protection for their Christian minorities; that would be culturally insensitive. We just give victims refuge as we give everyone refuge, assisting the Christian Exodus. Pakistani girl Rimsha Masih fled with her family to Canada in June 2013, after charges against her for blasphemy were dropped.

A man who could've been a poster image for Western multiculturalism was Patrick Sookhdeo, born in British Guiana to a Hindu father and Muslim mother before moving to Britain. He ruined it all by adopting Christianity, but not the West's postmodern, multicultural Christianity. In his 2007 book *Global Jihad: The Future in the Face of Militant Islam*, he warned that *"non-violent Islam is like a cone balanced on its point; it cannot exist in that state indefinitely but is bound… to give rise to violent elements."* White people's prejudice has nothing to do with it.

Anglican vicar Mark Durie, author of the 2010 book *The Third Choice: Islam, Dhimmitude and Freedom*, agreed that Islam is intrinsically violent. Persecuted religious minorities like Christians and the Falun Gong in China haven't become terrorists. Muslims are at least as violent in countries they dominate as they are in countries they don't; Muslim terrorism affects Muslim countries, too.

A 2013 report by the Pew Research Centre found that seventy-five percent of Muslims in Pakistan believed any Muslim renouncing Islam should be executed. So did forty-three percent in Bangladesh and forty-one percent in Iraq

Only one percent of Bangladeshis being Buddhist didn't deter twenty-five thousand Muslims in 2012 from reacting to a photograph posted on the Facebook website they considered offensive to Islam. They set fire to eleven Buddhist temples.

Begum Khaleda Zia was prime minister of Bangladesh from 1991 to '96 and from 2001 to '06. "I regret the continuing of massacre of Hindus and Buddhists in Bangladesh," she said, "but Bangladesh is an Islamic nation and not secular. Now, the Muslims are in majority here. Under the circumstances, if Hindus and

Buddhists want to live safely, they should either convert to Islam or go to India."

"The assumption is that, in Islam, there are a few rotten apples, not the entire basket," said Ayaan Hirsi Ali in 2015. "I'm saying it's the entire basket." She called in her book *Heretic* for a complete reformation of Islam, akin to the Protestant Reformation of the sixteenth century, rejecting the view that Muslims who don't engage in violence are moderate. "I think we're in a time now where we demand answers from Muslims and say, 'Whose side are you on?'"

Islam has no need to reform. The West likes it now.

Barack Obama lived in Indonesia as a child. As American president in November 2010, he visited, praising Indonesia's "spirit of religious tolerance" as an "example to the world."

While Obama spoke, retired Californian engineer Gregory Luke, a convert to Islam, languished in gaol on Lombok Island. The penultimate Sunday night in August, he'd entered a mosque to ask the loudspeakers not be so loud, whereby a group of local youths pushed him to the ground and pelted him with rocks. A mob chased him to his home and destroyed it, while police kept away. The only person charged for the night's events was Luke. "We recommend a sentence of seven months' gaol," prosecutor Baiq Nurjanah told the court in Praya, "as he is guilty of blasphemy and committing an act of hatred."

Some spirit, some example. In February 2011, Indonesians wanted a Christian man in West Java executed for blaspheming Islam. When a court sentenced him only to five years in jail, a thousand Muslims armed with machetes, sticks, and rocks attacked Christians, killing three and damaging several churches, screaming "*Allahu Akbar!*"

"The United States joins the vast majority of Indonesians in deploring the violence in Indonesia directed at members of the Ahmadiyah community that resulted in the deaths of three people and the wounding of several others over this past weekend," said American ambassador to Indonesia, Scot Marciel, in a statement, very politely. "We also note with concern the recent church burnings in Central Java." A mob of fifteen hundred Muslims had set two churches alight and ransacked a school during a previous rampage. "We encourage the Indonesian government to continue to foster tolerance and protect the rights of all communities."

It was all very little aside the military action we'd undertaken to protect Kosovars from Serbs, threatened to undertake to protect Albanians from Macedonians, and would soon undertake to protect Muslims from each other in Libya. "If this phenomenon continues," said Reverend Khalil Samir, an Egyptian Jesuit in Beirut, in 2010, "Christianity in the Middle East will disappear."

21. OUR LANDS OF OTHER PEOPLE

The land the West doesn't respect is our own. The concept of Christian land we've rejected since the Holocaust, although we understand the problem Christians can be.

When I was young, we knew well of the nineteenth-century Ghan cameleers who'd come to outback Australia from what had been the British colony of India. By early 2008, a National Library of Australia exhibition focused upon them being Muslims: Muslim Pioneers, no less. Afghans, Pakistanis, and the like coming to Australia from 1860 meant time was reason to feel comfortable about them, as European settlement in 1788 wasn't.

The talk was more personal and supportive about those Muslims than exhibitions about British colonisation now are. These were no imperialist invaders, as is the only history of European settlement we countenance, but brave men and women of the ilk that only a few generations earlier we'd seen our British forebears. I'm not sure how the museum curators knew so much about Ghans, as much as a century and a half later.

Much as we do of today's Muslims, the romantic vision of past Muslims omitted their crime and terror. It omitted the Battle of Broken Hill.

After arriving in Broken Hill in 1898, Mullah Abdullah was a cameleer, a halal butcher, and an imam. After a police court convicted him of slaughtering sheep on premises not licenced for slaughter, he and ice-cream vendor Badsha Mahommed Gool shot at a train to Silverton filled with picnickers on New Year's Day, 1915. Seventeen-year-old Alma Cowie and foreman William Shaw were killed. Seven others were injured. The two Ghans then killed Alfred Millard in his hut and wounded a policeman, before a ninety-minute gun battle with police and the military led to the death of James Craig while chopping wood nearby.

"*I must kill you and give my life for my faith,*" wrote Gool in a letter left behind, "*Allāhu Akbar.*" Gool had declared himself a subject of the Ottoman Sultan: the Ottoman Empire. Immigrant races prove especially dangerous during times of war.

Religion was also central to the *Faith, Fashion, Fusion: Muslim Women's Style in Australia* exhibition at the Powerhouse Museum, Sydney in June 2010. Accompanying the inescapable images of smiling Muslim women was text calling them Syrian, Lebanese, and Anglo Australian; we who'd been Australian had become Anglo Australian, without any say in it. Standing tall from the first display stand confronting us in the museum shop was a bright shining book about Islam.

In contrast was the Wiggles exhibition downstairs, which my family and I visited. A section concerned with the singers' fundraising work after the September 2001 terrorist attacks made no mention of Muslims. We judge Muslims by their clothes, not their terror.

That same day, I read the deputy mayor of Bankstown, Allan Winterbottom, explain why he thought his local council area had the highest unemployment rates in Sydney. "There are jobs out there but people have to want to work," he said. "I don't want to tell you what sort of people or nationality they are, but the culture is they get enough money to survive without working."

The suburbs he cited had high concentrations of Lebanese and Vietnamese. I saw no mention of Muslims until Keysar Trad complained that Winterbottom tarnished an entire community with a "very, very narrow view," and that Muslims suffered discrimination when applying for jobs. A heavyset man with a beard, it's hard to imagine a grey suit, blue shirt, and tie would've made Trad less menacing. "Certainly," he claimed, "people with a Muslim-sounding name are not given the same opportunities... as people with an Anglo-sounding name."

Trad was chairman of the Islamic Friendship Association of Australia. Friendship with whom wasn't clear. He spent several years speaking to the media and taking legal actions in the New South Wales Supreme Court, Administrative Decisions Tribunal, Anti-Discrimination Board, Human Rights Commission, Press Council, and other review bodies on behalf of Muslims. (We don't have so many factories anymore, but have no end of courts, tribunals, and review bodies.) Taking great offence at even the meekest of criticisms, his might've been a brittle self-certainty, but was self-certainty nevertheless: opportunism with the rights and money we made available.

He saw great virtue in his tirade against radio station 2GB during what he called "a peace rally" in Sydney in 2005. After presenter Jason Morrison responded the next day, Trad sued the station owners for defamation. His own star witness, Trad's evidence included a claim he didn't know who wrote the book *Mein Kampf*. Trad feigned careful thought before slowly recalling the author's name: Adolf Hitler. What consumes Jews and the West isn't so important to others.

Demonstrating at least to Trad the great bias of Australian courts, he lost his case. Undeterred by already huge legal costs, Trad appealed that decision. Sixteen lawyers stood in court the second Friday of June 2010, including the veteran defamation lawyer Clive Evatt, walking with the aid of a cane.

"His honour," said Evatt on Trad's behalf, of the judge at the first trial, "did not take into account that Australia is a multicultural society and the viewpoints of ethnic groups are recognised by the Australian community even though not all members of the community agree with them... His honour did not... even consider the likelihood the average citizen would recognise that the views expressed... were similar to beliefs shared by Muslims throughout the world, including Muslims in Australia."

Evatt recognised viewpoints differed between races, which don't cease when we admit them into our countries. There is no multicultural voice: no global consensus.

The case continued for eight years. Trad lost.

We don't normally compile or report data suggesting the size of modern-day Muslim populations in the West for fear of stoking people's prejudice, except in some other context. In 2010, Centre for Independent Studies research fellow Jennifer Buckingham reported the rise of religious schools in Australia due "*to an increase in the Muslim proportion of the population, due to a combination of immigration and high birth rates, as well as policy changes made by the Howard government which made it easier to set up new schools.*"

In 2008, Britain's leading judge, Lord Chief Justice Lord Phillips of Worth Matravers, said British courts should use sharia to resolve disputes between Muslims. A week later, Stephen Hockman Q.C., a former head of the Bar Council, warned that "otherwise we will find there is a very significant section of our society which is increasingly alienated, with very dangerous results."

Hockman presumed Britain was a society. In 2009, Citivas found eighty-five sharia courts already operating there.

While Australians debate recognition of sharia, it's already being enforced. When Christian Martinez woke in his apartment on Melton Street, Silverwater at one o'clock in the middle Sunday morning of July 2011, he found four men in his bedroom. Three men held him to his bed for half an hour while the fourth lashed him forty times with a cable.

'Lashed 40 times after bearded men appear in man's bedroom,' declared the *Sydney Morning Herald* newspaper headline the next day. (We have no qualms about reporting assailants' facial hair.) The intruders being at large, the article mentioned they were in their late teens or early twenties and *"of Middle Eastern or Mediterranean appearance."*

We learnt the following day that the victim was a recent convert to Islam; his first name might've already changed from being Christian without being reported. The lashings were his punishment for drinking alcohol with friends.

The first assailant charged was Tolga Cifci. His barrister Ertunc Ozen *"said his client was born and raised in Australia, had no criminal record and had strong family ties."*

The second was Wassim Fayad, whose lawyer Avni Djemal said his client worked two jobs to look after his six children. "He has no violence on his record." The case "would not be remarkable but for the motivations."

A month later, addressing our parish Anglican church home group on the last Sunday in August 2011, South Sudanese refugee Ajang Biar lamented the British leaving Sudan in 1956 as we don't lament the end of European empire. The northern Arabs immediately oppressed the southern Africans, making all schools Arabic and Islamic. A brutal civil war erupted, with not simply a handful of renegade Arabs but Arabs en masse destroying southern infrastructure and bombing Christian schools. (Nobody claimed a majority of peace-loving Muslims then.)

Conflicts and wars stretched along the line between Arabs and black Africa. Biar spoke of the struggle between Islam and Christianity in Sudan as a microcosm of a struggle worldwide, without appreciating the West's resolve to struggle only with our own. He feared Muslim races, while we fear Western prejudice. If Biar had been white, we'd have called him an Islamophobe.

Biar wanted Christians to help each other. That meant us helping South Sudanese rather than them helping us. His audience nodded, without thought of helping Muslims any less. We give refuge to both.

Some solution to the Sudanese Civil War had been separating the country into two, earlier that year. (While we pursue a West without borders, other races keep putting them up.) The Arab north remained the Sudan. The African, partially Christian, south became South Sudan, which allowed Muslims to worship as Christians couldn't in Sudan, said Biar. The former cathedral in Khartoum, Sudan, was a government office building. Fighting continued, but they all felt safer in separate countries.

Afterwards, we spoke. Biar questioned multiculturalism, mentioning the lashing of Christian Martinez. He went onto say suburban Lakemba, Auburn, and Lidcombe were already Muslim territory in Sydney. He said two years earlier, Muslims harassed a church there, forcing it to close so a Muslim school could buy and incorporate it. I'd never before heard the story, although later recalled Muslims complaining that a Sydney local council didn't let them expand the use of a church they'd bought.

I asked Biar whether Australia should continue accepting refugees. "Yes," he said, "but be careful." He showed me what he said was a bullet scar on his arm and mentioned other injuries, supposedly proving he was a genuine refugee. His implication was that others weren't.

Still, I shouldn't read too much in Biar's words. I asked him about crime by Sudanese in Australia; any common Christianity hadn't kept them from assaulting, raping, and murdering us. "They were building gaols before the Sudanese came," said Biar, as if to say there'd already been crime so we shouldn't complain about more. He blamed the lack of services; Sudanese crime was our fault for not giving them even more than we already did. Acknowledging "one in a hundred" rotten Sudanese, he'd taught New South Wales police about working with Sudanese.

Muslims aren't the only parallel societies in the multicultural West. After legal academic Andrew Fraser and immigration minister Kevin Andrews had several years earlier spoken publicly of crime by Sudanese, Biar told Sudanese not to feel offended. "Prove to them you have I.Q.," he told them; they should prove their intelligence. He claimed to me that his leadership reduced

Sudanese crime. "They listen to me."

Sudanese social structures are racial, not religious. They aren't listening to white people. "Are you a country within a country?" I asked him.

"No," he said. "We work within the Australian system. The system brought us here. It has been good to us. You don't destroy the pot."

The pot of Western gold is unlike any other in history, created by our forebears but, rejecting their racism and nationalism, freely given by us to other races. Biar was like all the smarter immigrant leaders, wanting not to lose the pot too soon. For as long as we give them so much, they have reason to be civil. They'll lose their reason not to be a country within a country when the pot of gold exhausts.

Biar lived in Engadine, a rare remnant of almost-white Australia. Cities and suburbs throughout the West had been like the Sutherland Shire, when the first few immigrants came.

There's no pot in South Sudan. A few months later, up to eight thousand heavily armed fighters from the Lou Nuer tribe set off towards Pibor, hometown of the Murle. Fifty thousand Murle fled but Joshua Konyi, commissioner of Pibor county and a Murle, said the Lou Nuer still killed almost a thousand men and more than two thousand women and children. They abducted more than a thousand children and took more than three hundred thousand cows; cattle rustling had long been a feature of conflict between them. Any religion the two tribes shared didn't matter to them (although might've mattered to the cattle).

Among the fearmongers who've long warned about the impact of growing Muslim populations in the West was Jewish historian Raphael Israeli. "When the Muslim population gets to a critical mass you have problems," he said in 2007.

The same can be said of any minority race. My experiences of Humphrey have all been good, but he's been the only black person around. My experiences weren't so good in the black blocks of Baltimore.

"Where there are large Muslim populations who are prepared to use violence," continued Israeli, "you are in trouble. If there is only one or two percent they don't dare to do it – they don't have the backing of big communities. They know they are drowned in the environment of non-Muslims and are better behaved." He went onto say French police were scared to enter Muslim districts, where militants demanded anti-Semitic policies and opposition to Israel. (Increasingly, so are multiculturalists.) "French people say they are strangers in their own country. This is a point of no return."

Keysar Trad rejected Israeli's warnings. "Not only religious clerics need to be screened before entering Australia, but also academics," he said. "This type of academic does nothing but create hatred, suspicion, and division… We should review not only what the man has said, but also those who have sponsored him, to see if they endorse those comments."

Trad was referring to the Shalom Institute of the University of New South Wales and the Australia–Israel Jewish Affairs Council. If he was suggesting we can't trust what Jews say about anti-Semitism, we don't impose such a restriction upon Muslims alleging anti-Muslim prejudice.

Readers' responses to a 2010 Australian news report about the Muslim baby boom were most telling. One saw a quarter of the population being Roman Catholic as a bigger bar to multiculturalism than a smaller proportion of Muslims. Another, 40 Degrees S, dismissed conflicts with Muslims as being like Europe's Wars of Religion four hundred years earlier. The fault lay with religion in general.

Scarface believed we're the problem. "*The tone of this piece is highly offensive. Muslims are not the enemy: it's the intolerant among us who treat those who are different as dangerous that inflame the divisions in our society.*" (We're supposed to ignore the divisions.) "*It reminds me of when Pauline Hanson warned us we were to be 'swamped by Asians'. My response at the time was, 'So what?' What difference does it make? Aren't we a tolerant society, welcoming of all?*"

We understand Jews wanting to live by their religion and other culture. We understand Sikhs, Buddhists, and other immigrants wanting to live by theirs.

It's reasonable for Muslims to want to live by sharia. Whether that's traditional, religious, secular, or some hybrid of them, is for Muslims to decide. When their numbers are large enough, they'll decide the extent to which they impose it upon us. They'll want laws protecting their families and faithful from what they consider corrupting influences, even if we don't.

"If Muslims ever become a majority in the United States," Ibrahim Hooper of the Council on America–Islamic Relations told

Michael Medved's radio programme in October 2003, "it would be safe to assume that they would want to replace the U.S. Constitution with Islamic law, as most Muslims believe that God's law is superior to man-made law."

22. EURABIA

"*French minority groups tend to have alien values,*" wrote Michel Gurfinkiel, editor in chief of *Valeurs Actuelles* news magazine, in 1997, "*to think of themselves as a new nation, and even to have hopes of superseding the present Judeo–Christian nation of France.*"

In 2010, the British Broadcasting Corporation reported Islamic schools teaching sharia in Britain. "*For thieves their hands will be cut off for a first offence,*" said a textbook for fifteen-year-old children, "*and their foot for a subsequent offence. The specified punishment of the thief is cutting off his right hand at the wrist. Then it is cauterised to prevent him from bleeding to death.*" The punishment for homosexual acts was death by stoning, burning with fire, or throwing off a cliff.

It was geographically Britain, but the schools were part of the Saudi Students Clubs and Schools in the U.K. and Ireland organisation. "I have no desire or wish to intervene in the decisions that the Saudi government makes in its own education system," said British education minister Michael Gove.

The children being taught Jews were conspiring to take over the world attracted Gove's attention. "But I'm clear that we cannot have anti-Semitic material of any kind being used in English schools," he said. Britain's education authority, "Ofsted will be reporting to me shortly." In our pursuit of a global civilisation, Western countries exist only to the extent necessary to eradicate prejudice against everyone but us.

New Year's Eve headed into 2014, Muslims destroyed a thousand cars in their annual protests across France. The French were far more concerned about Muslim comedian Dieudonné M'bala M'bala's recent joke about a Nazi Israeli settler. In the resulting furore, he complained about the Jewish lobby in France and the American–Zionist axis. Dieudonné, whose father was from Cameroon, had begun his career with Jewish comic Élie Semoun campaigning against French people's racism. French authorities set about banning his forthcoming stage show for anti-Semitism.

Jews who'd worked so hard to prevent the West committing

another Holocaust are facing the first sense of a Holocaust from Muslims. "This new hatred comes from Muslim immigrants," said Judith Popinski in 2010. The widow, eighty-six years of age, had come to Sweden from a Nazi concentration camp more than sixty years earlier. "The Jewish people are afraid now." She'd spoken to schoolchildren about the Holocaust, but Muslim children ignored her. Schools in Muslim areas had stopped inviting Holocaust survivors to speak. "Some Swedish politicians are letting them do it, including the mayor. Of course, the Muslims have more votes than the Jews."

This was the society that Prime Minister Fredrik Reinfeldt was determined to defend. Jewry died in the death camps and can't die again.

Multiculturalism is achieving what Nazism failed to do: driving the Jews from Europe. Anti-Semitism is rising, but to blame Muslims for it would be Islamophobic.

In 2016, Britain's Labour Party suspended journalist Rod Liddle for writing that anti-Semitism is *"absolutely endemic"* among Muslims, *"an ingrained part of their unpleasant ideology."* Liddle had been a party member for thirty-seven years.

We don't imagine anyone but us carrying a Holocaust into effect. That presumption is Western arrogance, as is our arrogance to think we can strip Muslims of their anti-Semitism the same way we've been stripped of ours.

Unwilling to link prejudice with anyone but us, we focus upon our dwindling peoples. Even when acknowledging Muslim anti-Semitism in Germany in August 2014, research fellow Peter Ulrich at the Centre for Anti-Semitism Research at Berlin's Technical University blamed Germans. He saw "a kind of rebellion of people who are themselves excluded on the basis of racist structures."

While Ulrich blamed his race, and of much less interest to us, the Islamic State of Iraq and the Levant overran the Christian city of Qaraqosh, removing Christian Crosses, forcing Christians to become Muslims, and then beheading them. "We will raise the flag of Allah in the White House," it promised, before America began bombing Islamic State forces to protect not Christians but Yazidis. The Islamic State flag already flew outside the Will Crooks housing estate on Poplar High Street, east London.

Later that month, with Britain raising the risk of terrorism to severe, came news that the most common male name in Oslo was

Mohammed. "It is very exciting," declared Jørgen Ouren of Statistics Norway.

It was somewhat incongruous to learn about 2009 from former British prime minister Tony Blair that European governments understood more than their citizens the danger of Muslim terrorism. His government had engineered a threefold increase in the Muslim population of Britain since 2000. In 2009, the *Times* newspaper in London reported a *"Muslim population 'rising 10 times faster than rest of society',"* growing by more than half a million to almost two and a half million. The number of Christians fell by more than two million in the preceding four years, according to a collation of research by the Office for National Statistics.

When Adrian Michaels of Britain's *Telegraph* newspaper reported that higher rates of immigration than those officially reported meant one fifth of Europe would be Muslim by 2050, he didn't question immigration. He said Europeans needed to do more to assimilate Muslims.

We are the perfect hosts. Our challenge isn't to preserve our people, but to house and school immigrants before we die.

By 2010, Mohammed (through its twelve different spellings: Muhammad, Mohammad, Muhammed, Mohamed, Mohamad, Muhamed, Mohammod, Mahamed, Muhamad, Mahammed, and Mohmmed) was the most popular name for boys born in Britain. In the West Midlands, the spelling of Mohammed was single-handedly the most popular boy's name.

By 2013, the *Times* newspaper thought it was great that one tenth of babies born in England and Wales were Muslim, with the proportion of Muslims under five twice that of the general population. "This generation is very much British," said Sheikh Ibrahim Mogra, the assistant secretary-general of the Muslim Council of Britain. "They feel very much this is their home." It was no longer the English people's home. At Batley, West Yorkshire, *"pubs, hospitals, houses and public buildings"* had become *"Muslim private schools, madrassas, mosques and a Sharia court to satisfy rising demand from families."*

Along with immigration, high birth rates, and conversions to Islam was a growing willingness by Muslims to call themselves Muslim. War and terrorism strengthen their sense of Muslim identity, while further reducing the West's willingness to identify anyone as anything.

"The implications are very substantial," said Oxford University demographer David Coleman in 2009. "Some of the Muslim population, by no means all of them, are the least socially and economically integrated of any in the United Kingdom... and the one most associated with political dissatisfaction. You can't assume that just because the numbers are increasing that all will increase, but it will be one of several reasonable suppositions that might arise."

While white people worry about worldwide population growth, Coleman said Muslims would reap collective benefits from their increasing numbers. "In the growth of any population... voice is regarded as being stronger in terms of formulating policy, not least because we live in a democracy where most people in most religious groups and most racial groups have votes. That necessarily means their opinions have to be taken and attention to be paid to them."

The biggest Christian population was over seventy years of age. The biggest Muslim population was under four. "The groups with the strongest belief in the family and cohesion are those such as the Pakistanis and Bangladeshis," said Manchester University social geographer Ceri Peach. "They have got extremely strong family values, but it goes together with the sort of honour society and other kinds of attributes which people object to. So you are dealing with a pretty complex situation."

Peach cared only about the economy. He saw Muslims benefiting Britain's future labour market, sustaining the ageing white people.

We're certain immigrants will be as happy to work and pay taxes to support us as we've been to work and support them, but in 2013, preacher Anjem Choudary ridiculed the lives of British workers in secretly recorded addresses to three meetings of Muslims in Britain. "You find people are busy working the whole of their life. They wake up at seven o'clock. They go to work at nine o'clock. They work for eight, nine hours a day. They come home at seven o'clock, watch *East Enders*, sleep, and they do that for forty years of their life. That is called slavery."

Some revered Islamic figures only worked one or two days a year, Choudary proudly told thirty Muslims. "The rest of the year they were busy with jihad and things like that. People will say, 'Ah, but you are not working,' but the normal situation is for you to take money from the Kaffir," the non-believers. "So we take Jihad Seeker's Allowance. You need to get support." A father of four, Choudary claimed more than twenty-five thousand pounds a year in government benefits: eight thousand pounds more than British soldiers fighting the Taliban in Afghanistan. "We are going to take England. The Muslims are coming."

Choudary repeated the theme at a meeting of Muslims in Slough. "Now we are taking over Birmingham and populating it," he said. "Brussels is thirty percent, forty percent Muslim and Amsterdam. Bradford is seventeen percent Muslim. These people are like a tsunami going across Europe, and over here we're just relaxing, taking over Bradford, brother. The reality is changing." The new Europe won't be like the old. "Democracy, freedom, secularism, the parliament, all the MPs and the presidents, all the Kaffir's ideas, everything the people worship, we have to believe that they are bad and we have got to reject them."

"What ultimately do we want to happen to them?" he asked a community centre in Bethnal Green, east London, referring to Prime Minister David Cameron and others as the Shaitan: the Devil. "Maybe I'm the only one who wants the Shaitan to be killed. The Shaitan should be finished. There should be no Shaitan."

Choudary was confronted with the recordings. "Many people in the Muslim community are on Jobseeker's Allowance and welfare benefits," he said, before flagrantly lying. "As a joke, I may say something about Jihad Seeker's Allowance. Clearly it is not a Jihad Seeker's Allowance. The word 'jihad' means struggle. It does not necessarily mean fighting. I have never said to anyone to kill anyone in this country."

The Islam 4 U.K. group, of which Choudary had been head, planned up to fifty thousand bright yellow stickers like those Muslims began posting on bus stops and street lamps around the London boroughs of Tower Hamlets, Waltham Forest, and Newham in 2011. *"You are entering a Sharia-controlled zone — Islamic rules enforced."* Tower Hamlets was among the parts of east London where women not wearing headscarves were threatened with violence and death.

"This is the best way for dealing with drunkenness and loutishness, prostitution, and the sort of thug life-attitude you get in British cities," explained Choudary. He'd come a long way from his student days, sleeping with several white Christian girls, smoking cannabis, drinking cider, and preferring to be called Andy. "This will mean this is an area where the Muslim community will not tolerate drugs, alcohol, pornography, gambling, usury, free mixing between the sexes – the fruits if you like of Western Civilisation." There would also be no music or concerts. "We want to run the area as a sharia-controlled zone and really to put the seeds down for an Islamic emirate in the long term."

The British government identified twenty-five areas around the country where violent extremism was a problem, but Waltham Forest Council leader Chris Robbins wasn't concerned. "People should not get the wrong idea about our borough because a handful of small-minded idiots, who do not live here, decide to deface our streets with ridiculous posters."

It would be perfectly natural for the Islamic dream of an Islamic state through North Africa, the Middle East, and western Asia to encompass other lands with large Muslim populations. Suggesting otherwise would be like saying it shouldn't include Turkey, Albania, or Lebanon because they'd been Christian. Once in a while, I encounter the term Eurabia to refer to Europe no longer European blending seamlessly into the Middle East.

Among its regular broadcasts of Friday sermons from Muslim clerics, the Hamas television station Al-Aqsa broadcast one the second Friday of April 2008 from Yunis al-Astal, also a member of the Palestinian parliament. "Very soon, Allah willing," he told his people, "Rome will be conquered, just like Constantinople was, as was prophesised by our prophet Muhammad."

Rome used to be Roman. It isn't yet Muslim.

"Today, Rome is the capital of the Catholics, or the Crusader capital, which has declared its hostility to Islam, and has planted the brothers of apes and pigs in Palestine in order to prevent the reawakening of Islam." (How little Israel prevented Islam's reawakening wasn't explained.) Al-Astal's destination was Rome. "This capital of theirs will be an advanced post for the Islamic conquests, which will spread through Europe in its entirety, and then will turn to the two Americas, and even Eastern Europe."

Other races see their generation's role being to prepare succeeding generations. (So do we, but not our succeeding generations.) "I believe that our children," said al-Astal, "or our grandchildren, will inherit our jihad and our sacrifices, and, Allah willing, the commanders of the conquest will come from among them. Today, we instil these good tidings in their souls – and by means of the mosques and the Koran books, and the history of our prophets, his companions, and the great leaders, we prepare them for the mission of saving humanity from the hellfire at whose brink they stand."

The speech, like scores, hundreds, or thousands like them, went unreported, except among Muslims it meant to inspire. I stumbled upon it from my Jewish friend Ian's website, along with others brazenly demanding death to Western infidels.

Endorsing author Sam Harris, Ayaan Hirsi Ali said in 2015 that "Sam realises that among religions, Islam is unique in its atrocity, that everything we said about Christianity and Judaism was hundreds of years ago. He calls Islam 'the mother lode of bad ideas,' which is extremely brave." Western Europe, she said, ignores the threat of self-segregating Islamic immigrants at its peril. "This is a transformation of the West as we know it."

If we don't move on from the Holocaust, closing behind us the gates of Auschwitz, rapidly changing demographics mean Europe and parts of North America and Australasia will become Muslim, with or without terrorism. "Make not three, but five children," Turkish president Recep Tayyip Erdoğan told Turks living in Europe in 2017, "because you are the future of Europe." We are delivering our countries to Allah.

History is written by the victors. The future will record that Allah delivered Europe to Muslims.

Western individuals care little for what doesn't affect us in our lifetimes, just so long as we have cuisines we want, maintain our ideologies of inclusion and equality, and assure our little selves we're good. We care even less what happens afterwards.

Instead, we fret about white people's prejudice. I imagine the last white person killing the second last in some self-righteous sense of self-defence, whereby we'll finish fighting World War II.

23. REDEFINING OUR FALLEN

Western soldiers, sailors, and airmen dead in ancient wars might've died for motivations we consider obsolete, but they died for something: their comrades beside them; their wives, children, and grandchildren, generations unborn. European peoples died by the millions for Patria, in the words of a war memorial in Hornsby. The memorial in Bathurst to the South African War from 1899 to 1902 was *"in memory of those who gave their lives for the empire."*

Our nationalist dead died for their countries, when their countries were their race. The two were synonymous. They died in our defence.

"They Died That We Might Live," says an old board hanging in the Returned Services League Club, Mittagong, of World War II. Men and women dead in their country's name can't have died to let their countries disappear, but to bequeath their countries to us.

Remembrance Day 2013, ninety-five years after the end of the Great War and sixty-eight years after the end of World War II, the *Australian Broadcasting Corporation News* website reported on the war remembrance services scheduled that day. *"At 74 and as a survivor of the London blitz,"* commented Me of Wherever at eight forty-two that morning, the first comment of the day, *"I still shed a tear for our hero's from all Nations. But I ask myself why did they bother to step up and die, when I look around and see we have been taken over by stealth the same type of people they fought against. I think, when will our politicians find the same kind of courage they had and do something to stop this? My love and respect to all our fallen hero's and to all those who still keep stepping forward's to die for what we believe in."*

The comment was still there when I read the article at about a quarter to eleven that morning, but moderators control websites. By lunchtime, the comment had gone.

"Lest We Forget," still breathe the war memorials our forebears left behind. Sombrely, we repeat those words each Remembrance Day. We don't forget old wars, but our honour to the fallen isn't so much, "We shall remember them." It's more along the lines, "We

shall redefine them." Lest We Remember.

Few things more readily symbolise the loss of our countries than the loss of our flags; that's the reason we lose them. Canada's controversial adoption of the Maple Leaf in 1965 might've appealed to Canadians rejecting their country's British heritage, but many a veterans organisation continued flying the Canadian Red Ensign. Their comrades didn't die for a tree.

In Australia, the first Anzac Day commemorations honoured Australians and New Zealanders in war. Ninety-five years after Anzac troops began dying at Gallipoli in 1915, journalist Ray Martin hosted a television debate about changing Australia's flag. "We need a flag that represents all of us in this incredibly successful multicultural country," he declared, "a flag that includes indigenous Australians." Martin wasn't indigenous. He wanted to remove the British Union Jack.

Don Rowe, president of the New South Wales Returned Services League, said having such a debate on Anzac Day was ridiculous. Before we had multiculturalism we had people, and that flag represented the people for whom our soldiers fought and died. Few people from other races fought in our armies, although it's become fashionable to speak of them out of all proportion to their numbers. Other races enjoying the benefits of our countries didn't make our countries any less our countries, not then.

Rowe's objections didn't perturb Martin, who claimed our soldiers fought and died for free speech: *his* free speech. Martin, who'd never fought, reasoned our soldiers died under a flag so he could change it.

No war memorial I've seen dedicated the dead to freedom of speech. Memorials that speak of freedom don't speak of freedom in abstract, but their people's freedom. For Australians and other British, it was Martin's freedom to be sure. He didn't care how he got it.

We're not so interested in freedom of speech for the people who fought, not when they're conveying the reasons they did. We're scornful towards anyone saying what we refuse to believe.

A year later, the morning of Anzac Day 2011, Jim Wallace sat with his elderly father. Wallace had been a Special Air Service commander before becoming managing director of the Australian Christian Lobby. His father was a veteran of the Siege of Tobruk and Battle of Milne Bay during World War II, who lamented that he couldn't recognise the country for which he fought. "*Just hope that as we remember Servicemen and women today,*" Wallace wrote on the Twitter website, "*we remember the Australia they fought for – wasn't gay marriage and Islamic!*"

The furore from people who'd never fought was immediate. "*What they fought for was freedom from prejudice and persecution,*" insisted one Twitter user, although his use of the third person pronoun made it clear he hadn't fought. "*For all Australians!*"

People who never went to war demanded to speak for those who did, and even for God. "*Those people fought and gave their lives to keep our nation democratic,*" wrote Outraged Australian, "*and free from hate and intolerance. On any day of the year this is an ugly and disgusting idea to even have, let alone state in public. Jesus would be ashamed of you. You should be ashamed of yourself too.*"

Wallace's father could no longer be relied upon to know the reasons he fought. We've decided he fought for something else altogether.

Personally, I had trouble imagining soldiers firing guns, sailors firing missiles, and pilots dropping bombs in the name of tolerance, until I read the vitriol set upon Wallace. It's incongruous to imagine our forebears went to war and died in opposition to prejudice, while we spend the rest of our time denigrating their prejudices. Michael for Freedom of Sydney called Wallace a "*vile hateful ignorant fool.*"

The most aggressive, abusive people aren't the most racist. They're people most opposed to white racism: our most vociferous foes.

By that night, there were more than three hundred responses to Wallace's comments on the *News Limited Network* website alone. Wallace "*unreservedly*" apologised, writing "*this was the wrong context to raise these issues.*" (There is no right context, not anymore.) "*ANZACs mean too much to me to demean this day, not intended... I would never want to politicise Anzac Day – never my intention.*"

He'd made the mistake of writing spontaneously where strangers read. "*The interpretation that is being made of this – that I am saying that Australians didn't fight for everybody – is totally wrong. I was a soldier. I know full well how soldiers feel and think. Anyone defending Australia or serving in the defence force is doing it for every Australian.... Even in the time of Anzacs, there were not only gays but Afghans in Australia.*" (I wondered how much of what Wallace said was sincere and how much was him trying to escape.) *"But I think the Judeo–Christian heritage that framed the nature of Australia that these fellows fought for is very important. We should be trying to preserve it."*

He explained his error. *"And my ill-timed Twitter was just reflecting the nature of Australia that people fought for is different and I think it's being redefined all the time."* Indeed it was.

Those who weren't there interpret past wars in the image of our ideals – what we want wars to be – as the people who fought never did. Our soldiers wounded or killed don't come into it. We impute reasons for their sacrifice the dead never imagined. Our forebears died for whatever we want.

When we redefine the reasons our forebears went to war, we're doing more than rejecting their values and motivations. We're giving them ours, imposing upon them our states of mind, although we'd never fight for them. We don't put ourselves out for anything.

We think it's our right, but it's our capacity: a freedom we have, because our forebears fought and died. So they become the reasons they did, however much they would have hated what we're doing.

They defended their cultures to the death in war for us to surrender them in peace. They may well have refused to fight for our countries had they known we'd give our countries away. They'd not have died for a race that came to reject them.

Wallace's critics claiming to be former servicemen, at least that I read, didn't mention their wars. The comments of those defending Wallace included most of those saying they'd fought or knew people who had. *"Maybe my grandfather and great grandfather were rednecks and bigots,"* wrote Proud of Canberra, *"but I had the privilege of knowing both of them and I know they did not risk their lives in Africa and France for gays or Islam. They would be horrified of the Australia of today with noisy minority groups dictating to the general population as to how they think and what to believe in. They were both fine men that served this country (as it was) to their best. I miss them both."*

In spite of Martin's confidence we're so successfully multicultural, Waverley Municipal Council banned the Australian flag from flying over the iconic Bondi Beach Pavilion on New Year's Eve 2006 for fear it would incite violence. "The Australian flag was used by both sides as a symbol around which to perpetrate racial violence," explained councillor George Copeland, referring to recent riots. "The people from Lakemba burnt the flag, and the

Cronulla people swathed themselves in it while pounding people." They were his raceless way of describing Arabs and Australians, although he only accused Australians of hitting anyone. Arabs, he suggested, falsely, only burned flags. "We didn't want to wave a red rag in front of either side on New Year's Eve."

Mayor Mora Main focussed less upon the risk of violence. "It's just that Bondi is not a ceremonial place," she said. "It's a place for recreation." Yet, the Aboriginal flag flew.

Being barred from flying our flags because of the offence they cause other races brings home that we're discarding the countries for which our forebears thought they fought. Logan City Council banned former soldier Aaron Wilson from flying the Australian flag outside his home in Eagleby in 2008 because a neighbour found it offensive, before public protest led the council to back down. "*I have neighbours with dogs that bark incessantly*," wrote one reader of the *Courier Mail* newspaper, "*and which the council states they 'can do nothing about the issue', and yet they can persecute a patriotic ex-soldier for displaying a public symbol of support for our brave sons and daughters currently serving in Iraq and Afghanistan.*"

Public outcry also led Denair Middle School to revoke its order to thirteen-year-old Cody Alicea that he remove the American flag from his bicycle in 2010. The boy's grandfather Robert, a veteran, said the school was concerned about racial tensions and uprisings.

In 2012, an Australian government review found celebrations of the coming centenary of Anzac Day 1915 could cause divisions in multicultural Australia. Other races' histories and remembering their dead aren't a problem.

"Nakba Day ought to be regarded as a day which, like Anzac Day, Christmas Day, or Australia Day, is referable to a particular date which is not movable," explained Judge Christine Adamson of the New South Wales Supreme Court, allowing the Arab march to proceed the third Tuesday evening of May 2012. "I do not regard it as reasonable to expect persons commemorating a particular date to defer or bring forward its commemoration so that it can be commemorated on a weekend. The date is the product of history."

Adamson noted the likely inconvenience to Sydney commuters. "If one's purpose were to disrupt commuter traffic, one could hardly choose a better time or place," she acknowledged, but refusing the protest "would be inhibiting... the right to freedom of expression and assembly. It will present a significant challenge to police officers to keep the peace and ensure the public assembly does not cause a breach of the peace.... It is the nature of a protest that others will be affected and their routines will be interrupted."

Ray Martin was right. Our soldiers did die for freedom of speech, but not ours. Dying for ours would be nationalistic. They died for tolerance, but only ours.

The night our local scout troop held its 2010 Christmas drinks, I met Cameron's father, who'd fought in World War II. "I can't help but think we've let you down," I told him.

The old man replied as if I'd said what he'd often thought, or the old soldiers often said among themselves, but he knew he could say little. "It's interesting you say that."

No other races so glibly redefine the reasons of those who fought and died for them as the West now does, but we have to redefine their sacrifices. If we don't, our boys and girls died for nothing in war.

Our forebears were never willing to surrender as much as we're sacrificing for the sake of our ideals. No other race is willing now. We should learn from the past, but not remain there. Only then can we confront the reality of the present and risks of the future. If we're not willing to defend ourselves, we're willing to be destroyed.

People consumed by their individualism might not care about saving their race and culture until they realise the benefits their race and culture are to them, but there is something uncommonly evil about people wilfully erasing their race and culture. It took two wars and a holocaust to bring the West to this point. It might take something similar for us to recover.

BIBLIOGRAPHY, REFERENCES

Articles

Abdelkader, Engy, '5 Myths About American Muslims 10 Years After 9/11,' *The Huffington Post* website, 8 September 2011.

Allard, Tom, 'Portrait of a bomber: nice, but he was easily led,' *The Sydney Morning Herald* newspaper, 11 August 2009.

Anonymous, 'Life for Muslims Americans after 9/11,' *GateHouse News Service* published in the *Advocate Tribune (Granite Falls News)*, 8 September 2011.

Awad, Marwa, 'Egypt Salafi urges U.N. to criminalize contempt of Islam,' *Reuters* news service, 22 September 2012.

Banham, Cynthia, 'ALP split on death penalty stance,' *The Sydney Morning Herald* newspaper, 21 October 2008, quoting Melissa Parke.

Barns, Greg, 'Anti-Muslim protest takes Cronulla to the Gold Coast,' *Crikey* daily mail, 2 December 2008. Greg Barns, 'Teacher's s-xual relationship treated like murder,' *Crikey* daily mail, 15 December 2008.

Basnett, Guy, 'We can't kick out 'Jihad' dad because kids are 'settled',' *The Sun* newspaper, 9 May 2010.

Bennhold, Katrin, 'Rapper in France is acquitted of libeling the police,' *International Herald Tribune* newspaper, 23 September 2008.

Benson, Simon, 'Aussies are waging jihad in Iraq: Fears terrorists will bring their twisted belief system home,' *The Daily Telegraph* newspaper, 19 June 2014.

Benson, Simon and *Australian Associated Press*, 'Sydney terror plot: Suspect arrived in Australia illegally on false passport,' *The Daily Telegraph* newspaper, 12 February 2015.

Bessems, Kustaw, 'Legal Stunts in the Wilders case,' *De Pers (The Press)* newspaper, 3 February 2009. Uncredited, 'Aussie cleric Feiz Mohamed calls for beheading of Dutch MP Geert Wilders,' *Agence France-Presse* news service published at *News Limited Network*, 4 September 2010.

Bloodworth, James, 'Why is the left so blinkered to Islamic extremism?' *The Independent* newspaper, 28 June 2013.

Bolt, Andrew, 'Let's be frank about immigrants,' *The Advertiser* (Adelaide) newspaper, 14 July 2010.

Bowcott, Owen and Kate Connolly, 'How Nazi guard Oskar Gröning escaped justice in 1947 for crimes at Auschwitz,' *The Guardian* newspaper, 17 July 2015.
Brown, Malcolm, 'Terrorists given maximum jail terms,' *The Sydney Morning Herald* newspaper, 15 February 2010, describing terrorists as zealots.
Bunyan, Nigel, 'Rochdale grooming trial: Police accused of failing to investigate paedophile gang for fear of appearing racist,' *The Telegraph* newspaper, 8 May 2012. Nigel Bunyan, 'Rochdale grooming trial: police knew about sex abuse in 2002 but failed to act,' *The Telegraph* newspaper, 9 May 2012.
Burke, Greg, 'Italy: Berlusconi's War of Words,' *Time* magazine, 28 September 2001.
Burleigh, Michael, 'Godless Europeans turn to cultural Christianity,' *The Australian* newspaper, 2 June 2006, referring to Eurabia.
Camber, Rebecca, "'No porn or prostitution': Islamic extremists set up Sharia law controlled zones in British cities,' *Daily Mail* newspaper, 28 July 2011.
Carlqvist, Ingrid and Lars Hedegaard, 'Sweden: Rape Capital of the West,' *Gatestone Institute*, 14 February 2015.
Chasmar, Jessica, 'Report: Muslim cleric invited to pray over fallen SEALs damns them during service.' *The Washington Times* newspaper, 9 May 2013.
Choahan, Neelima, 'Michael Leunig defends 'fascist epiphany' vaccination cartoon,' *The Age* newspaper, 19 August 2015.
Clark, Nick, 'Exclusive Brethren member on rape charge,' *Mercury* newspaper, 1 October 2009.
Colgan, Paul, 'Race profiles a blunted tool in fight against enemy within,' *The Punch* website, 4 August 2009. Rick Feneley and others, 'Open gate to terrorists,' *The Sydney Morning Herald* newspaper, 5 August 2009.
Connors, Bob, 'City Council Meetings to Begin with Muslim Prayers,' *NBC News Connecticut*, 7 September 2010. Bob Connors, 'City Council May Pull Plug on Muslim Prayer Idea,' *NBC News Connecticut*, 8 September 2010. Lauren Petty, 'Muslims Protest Moment of Silence,' *NBC News Connecticut*, 14 September 2010.
Correspondents in Geneva, 'Muslim minaret ban threatens Swiss harmony,' *Agence France-Presse* news service published at *News*

Limited Network, 29 October 2009. Uncredited, 'Kadhafi calls for jihad against Switzerland over minaret ban,' *Agence France-Presse* news service, 25 February 2010.

Correspondents in Kabul, "They were Christian missionaries and we killed them all,' gloats Taliban,' *Agence France-Presse* news service published at *News Limited Network*, 7 August 2010.

Correspondents in Washington DC, 'Special US prison units fill with Muslims,' *Agence France-Presse* news service published at *News Limited Network*, 6 March 2011.

Correspondents in Washington DC, 'US will 'never' be at war with Islam says President Barack Obama,' *Agence France-Presse* news service published at *News Limited Network*, 12 September 2010.

Dale, Amy, 'Palestinian Nakba Day protest in Sydney 'just like Anzac Day,' Supreme Court justice rules,' *The Daily Telegraph* newspaper, 16 May 2012.

Davidson, Helen, 'Isis doctor Tareq Kamleh: I don't care about losing Australian citizenship,' *The Guardian* newspaper, 21 June 2015.

Davies, Hannah, 'Logan City Council backs down over Digger's flag,' *The Courier Mail* newspaper, 9 October 2008.

Dolan, Andy, "What would happen if I had a scarf over my face?': Nightmare of Fireman Sam creator branded a racist over quip to airport security,' *Daily Mail* newspaper, 27 February 2012.

Doughty, Steve, 'Sharia law SHOULD be used in Britain, says UK's top judge,' *Daily Mail* newspaper, 4 July 2008. Steve Doughty, 'Former chair of Bar Council calls for sharia rules in English law,' *Daily Mail* newspaper, 5 July 2008.

Doyle, Jack, 'Mohammed is now the most popular name for baby boys ahead of Jack and Harry,' *Daily Mail* newspaper, 28 October 2010.

Dunn, Mark, 'Extremist group hires town hall for rant against democracy,' *Herald Sun* newspaper, 3 August 2010.

Evans, Rebecca and Paul Bentley, 'Terror raid 'led by white widow': Gang mastermind in veil barked orders at gunmen in mall massacre that left three Britons dead,' *Daily Mail* newspaper, 22 September 2013. Paul Bracchi and Rebecca Evans, 'From Home Counties prom queen to world's most wanted woman: How the 'White Widow' was obsessed with Islam even as a schoolgirl,' *Daily Mail* newspaper, 27 September 2013.

Ferran, Lee with contributions from *The Associated Press* and *BBC News*, 'Airline Employee Plotted With Al-Qaeda Leader, Prosecution Says,' *American Broadcasting Company News*, 2 February 2011.

Fife-Yeomans, Janet and Simon Black, 'Australia's Generation Jihad is homegrown,' *The Daily Telegraph* newspaper, 30 May 2013.

FitzSimons, Peter, 'Memo world: try saying sorry to avoid a sorry end,' *The Sydney Morning Herald* newspaper, 25 September 2001.

Forliti, Amy, 'Indictment: Somali gangs trafficked girls for sex,' *Associated Press* news service published at *Yahoo! News*, 9 November 2010.

Franklin, Matthew, 'Fraser was warned on Lebanese migrants,' *The Australian* newspaper, 1 January 2007.

Gardham, Duncan, 'Abu Qatada: Radical cleric to be released 'in next 24 hours',' *The Daily Telegraph* newspaper, 17 June 2008. Alan Travis, 'Abu Qatada release: Home Office fury as judge frees 'Bin Laden aide',' *The Guardian* newspaper, 6 February 2012. Tom Kelly, 'Qatada, the happiest man in England: Brother boasts of hate-preacher's delight as he is given a more expensive home (funded by the taxpayer, of course),' *Daily Mail* newspaper, 25 March 2012.

Gardham, Duncan and others, 'Sweden suicide bomber: Taimur Abdulwahab al-Abdaly was living in Britain,' *The Telegraph* newspaper, 12 December 2010.

Gee, Steve and Larissa Cummings, 'Council bans Australian flag,' *The Daily Telegraph* newspaper, 2 January 2006.

Gettleman, Jeffrey, 'Accounts Emerge in South Sudan of 3,000 Deaths in Ethnic Violence,' *The New York Times* newspaper, 5 January 2012.

Gurfinkiel, Michel, 'Islam in France: The French Way of Life Is in Danger,' *Middle East Quarterly* journal, March 1997.

Hale, Virginia, 'Just Hours Before Islamist Truck Terror, Hollande said Populism Is the Real Threat,' *Breitbart News*, 16 July 2016. Latika Bourke with *Reuters* news service, 'Bastille Day attack: Live with terrorism, says France's PM Manuel Valls,' *The Sydney Morning Herald* newspaper, 16 July 2016.

Hall, Melanie, 'Muslim preacher urges followers to claim 'Jihad Seeker's Allowance',' *The Telegraph* newspaper, 17 February 2013. Dan Sales, 'Vile Choudary: I've bin misunderstood,' *The*

Sun newspaper, 18 February 2013.

Halper, Daniel, 'Palestinian Sentenced to Death for Selling a Home to Jews,' *The Weekly Standard* magazine, 23 April 2012. Caroline Glick, 'The elephant of Jew hatred,' *The Jerusalem Post* newspaper, 19 April 2012.

Harding, Gareth, 'Analysis: Dutch politico's last interview,' *United Press International* news service, 6 May 2002. Ambrose Evans-Pritchard and Joan Clements in Amsterdam, 'Fortuyn killed 'to protect Muslims',' *The Telegraph* newspaper, 28 March 2003.

Harrington, Elissa, 'School Makes Boy Take American Flag Off Bike' and 'Officials Later Backtrack; Allow Boy to Fly Flag on Bike,' *Fox 40 News Sacramento, Stockton, and Modesto*, 12 November 2010.

Harrison, Dan, 'Islamic and Christian schools on the rise despite decline in religion,' *The Sydney Morning Herald* newspaper, 16 September 2010.

Haydon, Harry and Karen Morrison, 'Woolwich terror suspect revealed as Muslim convert known to MI5,' *The Sun* newspaper, 23 May 2013. Uncredited, 'Woolwich attack: My ex-boyfriend the terror suspect was a 'lovely, polite boy',' *The Telegraph* newspaper, 23 May 2013. Josh Halliday, 'Woolwich attack: BBC's Nick Robinson apologises after 'Muslim' description,' *The Guardian* newspaper, 23 May 2013. Deborah Snow and Nick Miller, 'DIY terror,' *The Sydney Morning Herald* newspaper, 25 May 2013.

Hayward, Andrea, 'Govt presents new multiculturalism policy,' *The Sydney Morning Herald* newspaper, 16 February 2011. Chris Bowen's speech, 'What makes multiculturalism great is mutual respect,' was published on 17 February 2011, without the words ascribed to Bowen in Hayward's article.

Henley, Jon, 'Antisemitism on rise across Europe 'in worst times since the Nazis',' *The Guardian* newspaper, 8 August 2014. Rajeev Syal, ''Jihadist' flag flown in east London,' *The Guardian* newspaper, 8 August. 2014.

Hernandez, Javier and Timothy Clary, 'Mosque Near Ground Zero Clears Key Hurdle,' *Agence France-Presse* news service published in *The New York Times* newspaper, 3 August 2010. Uncredited, 'Reject mosque suspicions, New Yorkers told,' *The Sydney Morning Herald* newspaper, 5 August 2010. Borzou Daragahi, 'Mosque debate fuels Muslim fury,' *Tribune Media Services* published at *The Sydney Morning Herald* newspaper, 24 August 2010.

Hillyard, Vaughn, 'Donald Trump's Plan for a Muslim Database Draws Comparison to Nazi Germany,' *NBC News Newton, Iowa*, 20 November 2015. Jeremy Diamond, 'Donald Trump: Ban all Muslim travel to U.S.,' *Cable News Network CNN*, 8 December 2015.

Hoft, Jim, 'French Artist's Calls For Peace End in Brutal Beating By Local Muslims,' *The Gateway Pundit*, 9 February 2015.

Hohmann, Leo, 'Feds admit 'terror-recruiting problem' among refugees,' *World Net Daily*, 20 April 2015.

Hohmann, Leo, 'New mantra to deny Islamic terror: 'Mental illness,' *World Net Daily*, 5 August 2016. G M Davis, *House of War: Islam's Jihad Against the World* (2015). David Kupelian, *The Marketing of Evil: How Radicals, Elitists, and Pseudo-Experts Sell us Corruption Disguised as Freedom* (2016).

Hohmann, Leo, 'Poll: Most U.S. Muslims would trade Constitution for Shariah,' *World Net Daily*, 24 September 2015.

Hope, Christopher, 'White Christian Britons being unfairly targeted for hate crimes by CPS, Civitas claims,' *The Telegraph* newspaper, 19 July 2010.

Ironside, Robyn, 'Catholic teacher Gerard Byrnes jailed for 10 years for raping, molesting 13 students,' *The Courier-Mail* newspaper, 4 October 2010.

Isaacson, Walter, 'Madeleine's War,' *Time* magazine, 9 May 1999. Deana Kjuka, 'Madeleine Albright's Scrap with Pro-Serbian Activists in a Prague Bookstore,' *The Atlantic* magazine, 29 October 2012.

Jenkins, Russell and Andrew Norfolk, 'Sex gang leaders jailed for raping young girls,' *The Times* newspaper, 7 January 2011. Melanie Phillips, 'While Muslim sexual predators have been jailed, it is white Britain's hypocritical values that are to blame,' *Daily Mail* newspaper, 10 January 2011.

Johnson, Boris, 'In the hundhaus just waiting to bite back,' *The Telegraph* newspaper, published at *the Sydney Morning Herald* newspaper, 4 February 2000. John Laughland, 'How the left has won the cold war,' *The Spectator* magazine, 5 February 2000.

Johnston, Cynthia, 'Analysis – Egypt's pig cull fans sectarian tension,' *Reuters* news service, India, 12 May 2009. Uncredited, 'Egypt YouTube pig cull clip sparks outrage,' *Agence France-Presse*

news service published on *Breitbart News*, 17 May 2009.
Jones, Kate, 'Judge slams 000 operator's reaction to Afghan woman's call for help days before her death at hands of husband,' *Herald Sun* newspaper, 8 April 2010.
Jopson, Debra, 'Homegrown jihad,' and 'Australia raising its own jihadists,' *The Sydney Morning Herald* newspaper, 4 February 2012. Debra Jopson, 'Family links strong in Australian cells,' *The Sydney Morning Herald* newspaper, 6 February 2012.
Kalish, Rachel and Michael Kimmel, 'Suicide by mass murder: Masculinity, aggrieved entitlement, and rampage school shootings,' *Health Sociology Review* journal, Volume 19, Issue 4, 2010. William Hamby, 'Connecticut Shooting, White Males, And Mass Murder,' *The Atlanta Atheism Examiner*, 14 December 2012.
Kassam, Raheem and Chris Tomlinson, "You Tweet A Lot… Watch Your Tone': Cops Threaten Dutch Man For Opposing Govt Mass Migration Plans,' *Breitbart News*, 27 January 2016.
Kennedy, Dominic, 'Rise in Muslim birthrate as families 'feel British',' *The Times*, 12 January 2014. Douglas Murray, 'Is the startling rise in Muslim infants as positive as the Times suggests?' *The Spectator* magazine, 10 January 2014.
Kerbaj, Richard, 'Muslim population 'rising 10 times faster than rest of society',' *The Times* newspaper, 30 January 2009.
Kidd, Jessica, 'Muslims gather to celebrate Eid Al-Fitr, feast to mark end of Ramadan,' *Australian Broadcasting Corporation News*, 17 July 2015. Uncredited, 'Gunman opens fire, kills four marines at US military centre,' *Agence France-Presse* and *Reuters* news services published at *Australian Broadcasting Corporation News*, 17 July 2015.
Klukowski, Ken, 'Breaking: Pentagon Confirms May Court Martial Soldiers Who Share Christian Faith,' *Breitbart News*, 1 May 2013.
Lay, Ken, 'We must be vigilant to keep all Victorians safe,' *The Age* newspaper, 20 September 2014. Craig Butt, 'One dead, two stabbed in Endeavour Hills,' *The Age* newspaper, 24 September 2014.
Leven, Rachel, 'Commerce considers labelling Arab Americans a disadvantaged minority,' *The Hill* website, 29 May 2012.
Leveque, Thierry and Nick Vinocur, France braces for annual New Year's car torchings,' *Reuters* news service published at *Yahoo! News*, 31 December 2010. Uncredited, 'Train across France

completes 'hell on wheels' journey,' *BBC Europe News*, 28 December 2010.
Levy, Mega, 'Outrage over Channel Nine cameraman's 'terrorist' slur,' *The Sydney Morning Herald* newspaper, 13 April 2010. James Whittaker, 'Nine cameraman lynched on Twitter: 'I'm not a racist,' *Crikey* website, 13 April 2010. Daniel Sankey and others, 'Revheads riot, trash Bob Jane store,' *Australian Associated Press* news service published in *The Age* newspaper, 20 March 2010. Uncredited, 'Channel Nine cameraman Simon Fuller sacked over 'f---ing terrorist' slur,' *News Limited Network*, 14 April 2010.
Lewis, Steve, 'Tackle 'extreme Islam before it's too late' Liberal MPs warn,' *Herald Sun* newspaper, 9 February 2011. Phillip Coorey, 'Senior Liberal condemns anti-Muslim 'bullies',' *The Sydney Morning Herald* newspaper, 23 February 2011.
Libermann, Rebecca, "Jealous' Finland gunman targeted ex-girlfriend's workmates,' *The Sydney Morning Herald* newspaper, 3 January 2010.
Liddle, Rod, 'I know who I'm supporting in the Corbyn-Hodge leadership contest,' *The Spectator* magazine, 3 May 2016. Aubrey Allegretti, 'Rod Liddle Suspended From Labour Over Spectator Piece On Muslims,' *The Huffington Post* website, 19 May 2015.
Lowe, Adrian, 'Porn-addict Christian father admits abusing 3-year-old,' *The Age* newspaper, 12 April 2011.
Mahdawi, Arwa, "Your in America' sets grammar fascists against fascists,' *The Guardian* newspaper, 28 November 2012.
Marcus, Caroline, 'Deputy mayor of Bankstown Allan Winterbottom thinks his residents are bludgers,' *The Sunday Telegraph* newspaper, 10 June 2012.
Markoe, Lauren, 'U.S. mosque report rapid growth in past 10 years,' *The Washington Post* newspaper, 1 March 2012. Joel Gehrke, 'Mosques in America nearly double since 9/11,' *Beltway Confidential* in the *Washington Examiner* newspaper, 29 February 2012.
Marsden, Sam, 'Numerous opportunities missed to protect 'first' white honour killing victim,' *The Telegraph* newspaper, 29 May 2012.
Masanauskas, John, 'New clamp on Muslim haters,' *Herald Sun* newspaper, 3 December 2011.
Masanauskas, John, 'Pay for our trips home - the Islamic Women's Welfare Association,' *Herald Sun* newspaper, 13 February 2012.

Masanauskas, John and Anne Wright, 'Muslims happy to be festive,' *Herald Sun* newspaper, 5 April 2011.

Masters, Chris, 'Inside Ivan Milat jail – the lowest circle of hell,' *The Daily Telegraph* newspaper, 18 September 2010.

McGeough, Paul, 'Christian lambs left to slaughter,' *The Sydney Morning Herald* newspaper, 8 January 2011. Uncredited, 'Sarkozy: Mideast Christians victims of 'cleansing',' *Middle East Online*, 7 January 2011.

McLellan, Ben, 'Muslim man refuses to stand in court due to religion,' *The Daily Telegraph* newspaper, 24 May 2014.

McLelland, Euan, "What should he shout, I'm blowing myself up for a generic terror cause?' Police are ridiculed for making grovelling apology to Muslims after fake ISIS suicide bomber shouting 'Allahu Akbar' during training exercise,' *Daily Mail* newspaper, 10 May 2016.

Media Release, 'Britons have become more generous in last year,' *Charities Aid Foundation*, 3 December 2013. Nicky Phillips with *Associated Press* news service, 'Australia tops list of charitable countries,' *The Sydney Morning Herald* newspaper, 10 September 2010.

Meo, Nick, 'Jews leave Swedish city after sharp rise in anti-Semitic hate crimes,' *The Telegraph* newspaper, 21 February 2010.

Michaels, Adrian, 'A fifth of European Union will be Muslim by 2050,' *The Telegraph* newspaper, 8 August 2009. Adrian Michaels, 'Muslim Europe: the demographic time bomb transforming our continent,' and 'We need policies for integrating Europe's immigrants,' *The Telegraph* newspaper, 8 August 2009.

Millar, Paul, "The weak, dirty dogs killed him on Ramadan',' *The Sydney Morning Herald* newspaper, 14 August 2010.

Miller, Joshua Rhett, 'Napolitano Apologizes for Offending Veterans After DHS Eyes Them for 'Rightwing Extremism',' *Fox News*, 16 April 2009.

Montgomery, Nancy and Michael Abrams, 'Prosecutor: Uka turned bus into 'deadly tunnel',' *Stars and Stripes*, 9 January 2012. Uncredited, 'Jihadist killer deserves life say prosecutors,' *Agence France-Presse* and *mdm* news services published at *The Local – Germany's News In English*, 9 January 2012.

Mroue, Bassem, 'Islamic State leader Abu Bakr al-Baghdadi implores Muslims to 'go to war everywhere' in new audio recording,' *Associated Press* news service published on the *News*

Corp Australia Network, 15 May 2015.

Murphy, Damien, 'Mosque opens its doors – and visitors open their minds,' *The Sydney Morning Herald* newspaper, 26 September 2011.

Murphy, Padraic, 'Man with al-Qaida links wins appeal to stay in Australia,' *Herald Sun* newspaper, 31 May 2010.

Nebehay, Stephanie, 'U.N. racism investigator to visit U.S. from Monday,' *Reuters* news service, 16 May 2008.

O'Loan, James, 'Australian International Islamic College teacher Pravin Chand says it banned national anthem,' *The Courier-Mail* newspaper, 5 December 2008.

Orange, Richard, 'Apartheid row at Norwegian school after it segregates ethnic pupils,' *The Telegraph* newspaper, London, 25 November 2011.

Owen, Glen, 'US shock jock Savage targeted 'to balance least wanted list,' *Daily Mail* newspaper, 25 July 2009.

Paddock, Barry, 'Police investigate hate crime after bacon found in Staten Island park during event marking end of Ramadan,' *New York Daily News* newspaper, 20 August 2012.

Parfitt, Tom, and Rob Virtue, 'Aylesbury child sex ring members jailed for 'grotesque' abuse of vulnerable schoolgirls,' *Daily Express* newspaper, 7 September 2015.

Percy, Karen, 'Muslim woman tells Melbourne Islamophobia forum 'racism hurts',' *Australian Broadcasting Corporation News*, 9 August 2015.

Perez, Chris and others, 'Oregon gunman singled out Christians during rampage,' *New York Post* newspaper, 1 October 2015.

Petherick, Sam and Lewis Pennock, '35-year-old man who attacked Bristol's Jamia Mosque with bacon dies in prison,' *Bath Chronicle* newspaper, 30 December 2016.

Petroski, William, 'Critics: Iowa terror drill portrays immigration foes as killers,' *The Des Moines Register*, 25 March 2011. Daily Mail reporter, 'U.S. anti-terrorism drill showing white supremacists shooting immigrants cancelled following threats to carry it out for real,' *Daily Mail* newspaper, 26 March 2011.

Pipes, Daniel, 'Hasan Akbar's Chilling Diary Entries,' *Middle East Forum* website, 14 April 2005.

Ralston, Nick and Stephanie Gardiner, 'Killing of the 'wild one' shatters peace of remote commune,' *The Sydney Morning Herald* newspaper, 17 April 2012.

Ramadge, Andrew, 'Australian Christian Lobby chief Jim Wallace's Anzac Day slur sparks outrage,' at *News Limited Network*, 25 April 2011. Outraged Australian commented at 4.17pm. Michael for Freedom of Sydney commented at 4.20pm. Proud Of Canberra commented at 4.16pm. Glenda Kwek, 'Christian leader sorry for Anzac tweets,' *The Sydney Morning Herald* newspaper, 25 April 2011.

Rehn, Alison, 'Funds to counter violence,' *The Daily Telegraph* newspaper, 2 April 2011. Uncredited, 'Cash for community groups to fight extremism,' *Australian Associated Press* news service published at the *News Limited Network*, 2 April 2011.

Roberts, Andrew, 'In defence of Il Duce,' *The Telegraph* newspaper, 2 July 2003.

Robinson, Georgina, 'Aussie mother jailed two years for 'insulting' Kuwaiti emir,' *The Sydney Morning Herald* newspaper, 22 April 2009.

Rosario, Justin, 'Kansas Doctor Under Attack For Not Forcing Ten Year Old Rape Victim To Give Birth,' *Addicting Info*, 9 August 2012.

Rundle, Guy, 'Rundle: violent xenophobia is off the leash in France,' *Crikey* daily mail, 21 March 2012. Ruth Sherlock, 'Gunman 'was ready to kill again',' *The Telegraph* newspaper, 21 March 2012.

Samandar, Lema, 'Al-Qaeda? Who? I had no idea, says David Hicks,' *Australian Associated Press* news service published at *News Limited Network*, 22 May 2011.

Schofield, Hugh, 'Dieudonne: The bizarre journey of a controversial comic,' *BBC News*, 31 December 2013.

Sheehan, Paul, 'Rudd's electoral cracks about to open further,' *The Sydney Morning Herald* newspaper, 9 June 2010, mentioning the Australian Human Rights Commission's use of a poster image of an Arab woman.

Shepherd, Tory, 'Australia does not have a 'way of life',' *The Punch* website, 8 February 2011. Rob Morris, 'Throwing the First Stone: State House District 91 Candidate Expresses Extreme Views on Gays,' *The Moore Daily* website, 10 June 2014.

Simons, Jake Wallis, 'City of Jihad: Chilling map reveals how Isis fanatics established network of terror where they could plot under noses of police,' *Daily Mail* newspaper, 23 March 2016, concerning Brussels.

Sirota, David, 'Let's hope the Boston Marathon bomber is a white American,' *Salon* website, 16 April 2013. Uncredited, 'Boston bombings suspect Dzhokhar Tsarnaev left note in boat he hid in, sources say,' *CBS News*, 16 May 2013.

Smith, Kyle, 'How Ahmed's clock became a false, convenient tale of racism,' *New York Post* newspaper, 19 September 2015.

Stolz, Greg, 'New bikie gang called Soldiers of Islam is gaining momentum on the Gold Coast,' *The Courier-Mail* newspaper, 13 December 2010.

Sullivan, Mike, with others, 'Woman in a veil knifed MP in gut,' *The Sun* newspaper, 15 May 2010. Mike Sullivan, 'British politician stabbed in the stomach as he meets female constituent,' *The Sun* newspaper published by *News Core*, 15 May 2010.

Townsend, Mark, 'Rise in UK use of far-right online forums as anti-Muslim hate increases,' *The Guardian* newspaper, 17 March 2019, especially eighth paragraph.

Tripp, Rob, 'Shafia murder trial: 'Filthy and rotten children,' Shafia says of his dead offspring,' *The Montreal Gazette* newspaper, 14 November 2011. Uncredited, "I am happy and my conscience is clear': father accused of honour killings says he would do the same again, court hears,' *Agence France-Presse* news service and *The Sydney Morning Herald* newspaper, 16 November 2011.

Uncredited, 'Anzac Day centenary has risks: review,' *The Sydney Morning Herald* newspaper, 26 March 2012.

Uncredited, "Beheading' poet wins conviction appeal,' *Reuters* news service, 18 June 2008.

Uncredited, 'Eight years jail for man who killed 4000,' *Agence France-Presse* news service published at *News Limited Network*, 4 December 2010, concerning Jorge Ivan Laverde.

Uncredited, 'European Court rejects UK terror search,' *Agence France-Presse* news service published in *The Sydney Morning Herald* newspaper, 13 January 2010, concerning section 44 of the Terrorism Act 2000.

Uncredited, 'Facebook used to organise Auburn racial riot – police,' *The Daily Telegraph* newspaper, 14 September 2009.

Uncredited, 'Father runs over daughter for becoming 'westernised': police,' *Associated Press* news service published in *The Sydney Morning Herald* newspaper, 22 October 2009.

Uncredited, 'FBI rules out terrorism in Utah shooting,' *Post Independent* newspaper, 14 February 2007.

Uncredited, 'France makes it harder to become French,' *France 24* news service, 29 December 2011, with data about French immigration.

Uncredited, 'French screen icon Bardot fined for anti-Muslim remarks,' *Agence France-Presse* news service published at *Brietbart News*, 3 June 2008.

Uncredited, 'Holder reassures Muslims of DOJ's anti-bias focus,' *Associated Press* news service published at *My Way*, 11 December 2010.

Uncredited, 'Indonesia seeks jail for American who allegedly pulled plug on mosque loudspeaker,' *News Limited Network*, 15 December 2010.

Uncredited, 'Iraqi in Denmark 'found suicide bombers,' *Agence France-Presse* news service, 3 May 2009.

Uncredited, 'JI is on the rise again: analyst,' *The Sydney Morning Herald* newspaper, 16 July 2009.

Uncredited, 'Kettle that looks like Hitler brews trouble for JC Penney,' *The Telegraph* newspaper, 28 May 2013.

Uncredited, 'Lashed 40 times after bearded men appear in man's bedroom,' *Australian Associated Press* news service published in *The Sydney Morning Herald* newspaper, 18 July 2011. Katherine Danks, 'Islam convert Christian Martinez allegedly lashed 40 times with an electrical cord as punishment for going to the pub,' *The Daily Telegraph* newspaper, 20 July 2011. Uncredited, 'Sydney sharia lashing case: second man in court,' *Australian Associated Press* news service published in *The Sydney Morning Herald* newspaper, 20 July 2011.

Uncredited, 'Manchester Arena Inquiry: Security 'fobbed off' bomber concerns,' *BBC News*, 20 October 2020. See also Uncredited, 'Manchester Arena Inquiry: Security 'did not approach bomber over racism fears',' *BBC News*, 28 October 2020.

Uncredited, 'Mohammed is most popular name in Oslo,' *The Local* website, quoting Jørgen Ouren, 29 August 2014.

Uncredited, 'Muslim Leaders Speak on Hindus National Security Integrity Threatened – Patriot Forum,' *World Hindu News*, 26 July 2014.

Uncredited, 'Muslim migrants riot in Athens,' *The Age* newspaper, 24 May 2009.

Uncredited, 'Muslim women not used to drinking walk free after attack on woman,' *The Telegraph* newspaper, 6 December 2011.

Uncredited, 'Parents say son was tormented for eating salami sandwich during Ramadan,' *The Daily Telegraph* newspaper, 13 November 2009.

Uncredited, 'Ray Martin ignites Anzac Day flag furore,' *The Sunday Telegraph* newspaper, 25 April 2010.

Uncredited, 'Religious intolerance 'the new racism',' *Agence France-Presse* news service published at *News Limited Network*, 1 July 2010.

Uncredited, 'Remembrance Day ceremonies to mark 95 years since end of World War I,' *Australian Broadcasting Corporation News*, 11 November 2013. Me of wherever commented at 8.42am.

Uncredited, 'Swedish women don headscarves after assault on Muslim,' *BBC News*, 19 August 2013.

Uncredited, 'Taliban executes seven-year-old 'spy',' *Herald Sun* newspaper, 10 June 2010.

Uncredited, 'UK students taught how to chop off hands: BBC,' *Agence France-Presse* news service published at *The Sydney Morning Herald* newspaper, 22 November 2010.

Uncredited, 'US 'deplores' religious killings in Indonesia,' *News Limited Network*, 9 February 2011.

Uncredited, 'Web kerfuffle stuns 'Hitler house' owner,' *Press Association* published in *The Sydney Morning Herald* newspaper, 2 April 2011.

Uncredited, 'Zimbabwe: Go back to England, Mugabe tells Whites,' *New Zimbabwean* newspaper, 5 September 2014.

United Nations Educational, Scientific and Cultural Organization press release, 'UNESCO Welcomes Release of French Journalists Christian Chesnot and Georges Malbrunot,' 22 December 2004.

Veiszadeh, Mariam, 'Ad campaign shows the real Islam,' *The Sydney Morning Herald* newspaper, 3 November 2011.

Vulliamy, Ed, 'A destiny worse than war,' *The Guardian* newspaper, 10 April 1993.

Waterfield, Bruno and Alex Spillius, 'Liege attacks: Lone gunman brings terror to streets of Belgian city with hand grenade attack,' *The Telegraph* newspaper, 13 December 2011. Uncredited, 'Two dead in racist shooting spree in Italy,' *Agence France-Presse* news service published by *Australian Broadcasting Corporation News*, 14 December 2011. Uncredited, 'Daily Telegraph, Washington

Post and Huffington Post Report Twitter Lie As Fact: Liege Killer 'Nordine Amrani Was Muslim Terrorist',' *Anorak* website, 14 December 2011.

Watson, Paul Joseph, 'DHS Video Characterizes White Americans as Most Likely Terrorists,' *Infowars* website, 21 July 2011.

Weeks, Linton, 'The Runner-Up Religions Of America,' *National Public Radio*, 22 June 2014. Robby Berman, 'I Always Thought the U.S. Was Christian/Jewish/Other. Nope. Check Out This Surprising Map,' *Upworthy* website, with the words, "*Our diversity may be our most fundamental strength.*"

Weir, Keith and Jeff Mason, 'Libyan Megrahi celebrations unsettle U.S., UK,' *Reuters* news service, 21 August 2009. Uncredited, 'Party at Lockerbie bomber's house,' *Agence France-Presse* news service, 23 August 2009.

Welch, Dylan, 'Australian's passport seized in Jordan,' *The Sydney Morning Herald* newspaper, 14 November 2011.

Welch, Dylan, 'Religious divide drives bikie war,' *The Sydney Morning Herald* newspaper, 16 February 2009. Dylan Welch, 'Bikie feud not religious, says leader,' *The Sydney Morning Herald* newspaper, 17 February 2009.

Wenham, Margaret and Alex Dickinson, 'Brisbane atheist and university lawyer smokes pages from the Koran and Bible in YouTube stunt,' *The Courier-Mail* newspaper, 13 September 2010.

Willsher, Kim, 'French ponder similarities between London, Paris attacks on soldiers,' *Los Angeles Times* newspaper, 26 May 2013. Henry Samuel, 'Paris police search for 'bearded man seen praying' before soldier attack, *The Telegraph* newspaper, 27 May 2013.

Woodlock, Rachel, 'Anti-Muslim tub-thumping helps extremists,' *The Age* newspaper, 23 March 2011.

Zwartz, Barney, 'Limit Muslim migration, Australia warned,' *The Sydney Morning Herald* newspaper, 16 February 2007.

Books

Ali, Ayaan Hirsi, born 1969, *Heretic: Why Islam Needs a Reformation Now* (2015). Maureen Callahan, "In Islam, they are all rotten apples': Ex-Muslim's call for religion's reboot,' *New York Post* newspaper, 22 March 2015.

CIA World Factbook, June 2008, estimated Lebanon's religious demography.

Darwish, Nonie, born 1949, *Cruel and Usual Punishment: The Terrifying Global Implications of Islamic Law* (2008), Thomas Nelson, especially page 219. Jim Holstun, 'Nonie Darwish and the al-Bureij massacre,' *The Electronic Intifada* (a name that says much of its Arab perspective), 26 June 2008, largely dismissed the book.

Durie, Mark, *The Third Choice: Islam, Dhimmitude and Freedom* (2010). Mark Durie, 'Muslim violence a fact, not prejudice,' *The Brisbane Times* newspaper, 25 March 2011.

Fukuyama, Francis, born 1952, *The End of History and The Last Man* (1993). Samuel Huntington, 1927-2008, 'The Clash of Civilisations?' *Foreign Affairs*, Council on Foreign Relations, Inc, Summer 1993.

Hanfstaengl, Ernst, with Brian Connell, *Hitler: The Missing Years*, 1957. Antoine Capet, 'The Creeds of the Devil: Churchill between the Two Totalitarianisms, 1917-1945,' *Finest Hour Online*, 31 August 2009.

Harris, Sam, born 1967, *Letter to a Christian Nation* (2006).

Harris, Sam, born 1967, *The End of Faith* (2004).

Hedges, Chris, *War Is a Force That Gives Us Meaning* (2002). Brendan O'Neill, 'Kony 2012 the bastard offspring of the liberal elite,' *The Drum* at *Australian Broadcasting Corporation*, 13 March 2012.

Hitler, Adolf, 1889-1945, *Mein Kampf*, translated into English by James Murphy, died 1946, Project Gutenberg of Australia, September 2002.

Islam for Dummies and *The Koran for Dummies*. Mehdi Hasan, 'What the jihadists who bought 'Islam for Dummies' on Amazon tell us about radicalisation,' *New Statesman* magazine, 21 August 2014. Emma Reynolds, 'ISIS recruits: Here's our 'Islam for Dummies', especially for you,' *News Limited Network*, 28 August 2014.

Kevin, Tony, born 1943, *Walking the Camino* (2007).

Klausen, Jytte, born 1954, *The Cartoons That Shook the World* (2009), Yale University Press. Mark Steyn, 'Salute Danna Vale,' *The Australian* newspaper, 16 February 2006. Andrew Hammond with Tim Pearce, 'Cartoon ruling may prompt 'Islamophobia',' *Reuters* news service, 24 June 2008. Correspondents in Oslo, 'Two found guilty in Norway over Muhammad cartoon plot,'

Agence France-Presse news service published at *News Limited Network*, 31 January 2012. Tim Blair, 'West should denounce vicious, primitive hatred,' *The Daily Telegraph* newspaper, 17 September 2012.

Marx, Karl, 1818-1883, *Contribution to the Critique of Hegel's Philosophy of Right* (written 1843, introduction published 1844, remainder published after Marx's death).

Orwell, George, born Eric Blair, 1903-1950, *1984* known also as *Nineteen Eighty-Four* (1949).

Popper, Karl, 1902-1994, *The Open Society and Its Enemies*, Routledge, volume 1 of 2 (1945).

Senior, Jayne, *Broken and Betrayed: The true story of the Rotherham abuse scandal by the woman who fought to expose it* (2016), Pan Macmillan. Rob Preece and Jack Doyle, 'Police turned a blind eye to sex grooming gangs for more than a decade, confidential files reveal,' *Daily Mail* newspaper, 25 September 2012. Uncredited, 'Inquiry exposes 1,400 cases of sexual and mental abuse of children in English town of Rotherham,' *Australian Broadcasting Corporation News*, 27 August 2014.

Sookhdeo, Patrick, *Global Jihad: The Future in the Face of Militant Islam* (2007).

Tzu, Sun, 5th century BC, *The Art of War*. Mark Thompson, 'The Fort Hood Report: Why No Mention of Islam?' *Time* magazine, 20 January 2010. Catherine Herridge and others, 'Lawmakers Blast Administration For Calling Fort Hood Massacre 'Workplace Violence',' *Fox News*, 7 December 2011. Byron York, 'Journalists urged caution after Ft. Hood, now race to blame Palin after Arizona shootings,' *The Washington Examiner* newspaper, 9 January 2011. Molly Hennessy-Fiske, 'Ft. Hood shooter received glowing evaluations before attack,' *Los Angeles Times* newspaper, 24 August 2013.

Vegetius (Publius Flavius Vegetius Renatus), late 4th century, *Epitoma Rei Militaris* (5th century), cited in the film *The Punisher* (2004).

Essays

Millet, Richard, '*Éloge Littéraire d'Anders Breivik*' (Literary Elegy of Anders Breivik, 2012). Bruce Crumley, 'French Essayist Blames Multiculturalism for Breivik's Killing Spree,' *Time* magazine, 28

August 2012. Daniel Piotrowski, 'Biggest moments of 2011,' *The Punch* website, 2 December 2011. Valeria Criscione, 'Norway killer Anders Behring Breivik legally insane, say experts,' *The Christian Science Monitor*, 29 November 2011.

Films

Agora (2009), written by Alejandro Amenábar and Mateo Gil, reviewed in *Variety* magazine, 18 May 2009.
Back to the Future (1985), written by Robert Zemeckis and Bob Gale.
Black Hawk Down (2001), based upon the 1999 book by Mark Bowden, born 1951.
Day Will Dawn, The (1942), based upon a story by Frank Owen, 1905-1979.
Harry Potter and the Deathly Hallows: Part 1 (2010), based upon the 2007 novel by J.K. Rowling, born 1965. Pat Hurst, 'Brother jailed for attack on Potter star,' *Press Association* published in *The Sydney Morning Herald* newspaper, 23 January, 2011.
Harry Potter and the Order of the Phoenix (2007), based upon the 2003 novel by J.K. Rowling, born 1965.
Illusionist, The (2006), based upon the Steven Millhauser, born 1943, short story, 'Eisenheim the Illusionist.' *A Short Insight into The Illusionist*.
Innocence of Muslims (2012) seems not to exist beyond a trailer. Ilya Gridneff and Rachel Browne, 'Police gas Sydney protesters,' *The Sydney Morning Herald* newspaper, 15 September 2012. Ilya Gridneff and *Australian Associated Press* news service, "Horrified': O'Farrell shocked by Sydney Muslim protests,' *The Sydney Morning Herald* newspaper, 16 September 2012. Paul McGeough, 'Light the touch paper and stand back,' *The Sydney Morning Herald* newspaper, 16 September 2012. Uncredited, 'Sydney protest not face of Islam: Abbott,' *The Sydney Morning Herald* newspaper, 16 September 2012. Mohamad Tabbaa, 'He's my brother – why angry Muslim youth are protesting in Sydney,' *The Sydney Morning Herald* newspaper, 19 September 2012. Mike Carlton, 'Lame old hobby horses and other beasts,' *The Sydney Morning Herald* newspaper, 22 September 2012. Guy Taylor, 'Muslim-led nations seek global ban on insults of Muhammad.' *The Washington Times* newspaper, 24 September 2012. Toby

Harnden, 'Obama tells United Nations it is 'time to heed the words of Gandhi', condemns 'disgusting' anti-Islam video and insists 'Muslims have suffered the most at the hands of extremism',' *Daily Mail* newspaper, 25 September 2012.

Jack Ryan: Shadow Recruit (2013), by Adam Cozad and David Koepp, based upon the screenplay *Dubai* (2007) by Adam Cozad.

O.H.M.S. (1937), written by Lesser Samuels and Ralph Bettison.

Patton (1970), based upon Ladislav Farago, 1906-1980, *Patton: Ordeal and Triumph* (1963) and Omar Bradley's memoir *A Soldier's Story* (1951).

Star Wars (1977), written by George Lucas.

Submission (2004), directed by Theo Van Gogh, written by Ayaan Hirsi Ali.

Truth about Saturday Night, The. Telegraph reporters, 'Muslim 'vigilantes' confront Londoners in name of Islam,' *The Telegraph* newspaper, 17 January 2013. Telegraph reporters, 'Muslim Patrol: thugs abuse man in second 'vigilante' video,' *The Telegraph* newspaper, 22 January 2013.

V for Vendetta (2005), written by Larry and Andy Wachowski, based on the graphic novel *V for Vendetta* (1982-1988) written by Alan Moore. Charlie Spiering, 'Photo: Egyptian rioters were wearing Guy Fawkes masks,' *The Washington Examiner* newspaper, 12 September 2012.

Valkyrie (2008), written by Christopher McQuarrie and Nathan Alexander.

World Trade Centre (2006), written by Andrea Berloff.

Judgments

Trad v Harbour Radio. Paul Sheehan, 'Explosive argument behind Trad's defamation reasoning,' *The Sydney Morning Herald* newspaper, 14 June 2010.

Radio Programmes

Lambie, Jacqui, 'Australia needs to have better scrutiny vetting refugees,' *Radio National Breakfast*, Australian Broadcasting Corporation, 18 November 2015.

Television Programmes

Australia: You're Standing in It (1983-1984).
Civilisation: Is the West History? (2011). My late Jewish friend Ian told me it said some things similar to my writing.
Devil's Advocate (2009). Scott Roxborough, 'Dutch TV show exonerates Osama bin Laden,' *The Hollywood Reporter*, 9 April 2009.
East Enders (1985 onwards).
Hatfields & McCoys (2012).
Islamic Invasion of Europe, An (2007).
Perfect Terrorist, A (2011), broadcast as part of *The Cutting Edge* programme on 31 January 2012. Ian Gallagher, "I was told to kill to my last breath': Captured terrorist's account of Mumbai massacre reveals plan was to kill 5,000,' *Mail on Sunday* newspaper, 30 November 2008. Damien McElroy, 'Mumbai attacks: Jews tortured before being executed during hostage crisis,' *The Telegraph* newspaper, 2 December 2008. Rina Chandran, 'Lawyers refuse to defend suspected gunman,' *Reuters* news service in Mumbai, 12 December 2008. Ben Doherty, 'Terrorist hanged over Mumbai massacre role,' *The Sydney Morning Herald* newspaper, 22 November 2012.
Q&A (2008 onward). Eleni Hale, 'Jihadists celebrating Victoria fires; taking joy in the scenes,' *Sunday Herald Sun* newspaper, 15 February 2009. Peter Chambers, 'I survived Marysville for an orgy of ocker self-love,' *Crikey* website, 19 February 2009. Uncredited, 'Black Saturday arsonist guilty on all counts,' *The Sydney Morning Herald* newspaper, 20 March 2012.
Seinfeld (1989-1998), especially 'The Soup Nazi' (1995). Patrick McDonald, 'Interview: Larry 'The Soup Nazi' Thomas for 'Mind Over Mindy',' *Hollywood Chicago* website, 29 July 2014.
South Park (1997 onwards). Uncredited, "'Muhammad' now a dirty word on 'South Park',' *Hollywood Reporter*, 22 April 2010. Uncredited, 'Man jailed for South Park death threats,' *Associated Press* news service published at *The Sydney Morning Herald* newspaper, 24 June 2012.
West Wing, The (1999-2006). Ben Shapiro, born 1984, *Primetime Propaganda* (2011). Mark Lawson, 'A liberal dose of laughter,' *The Guardian* newspaper published in *The Sydney Morning Herald* newspaper, 2 July 2011. The episode 'Isaac and Ishmael' was

broadcast on 3 October 2001.

ABOUT THE AUTHOR

Simon Lennon has travelled throughout Europe, America, Australasia, Asia, and the South Pacific, seeing how similar European peoples are to each other (wherever we live) and how different we of the West are to everyone else. He has university bachelor's degrees in science and law and university master's degrees in commerce and business. He is married with six children.

His non-fiction collection *The West* comprises the following sixteen books:

Mending the West
The Unnatural West: An Overview
The Tribeless West: An Overview
The Homeless West: An Overview
The Vanishing West: An Overview

Individualism
Western Individualism
The End of Natural Selection
The Need for Nations

Identity
People's Identity: Race and Racism
Of Whom We're Born: Race and Family
Biological Us: Gender and Sexuality

Nationalism
A Land to Belong: Nationalism
The Failure of Multiculturalism

Cultures
Reclaiming Western Cultures
Christendom Lost
Aiding Islam

He is also the author of another non-fiction book, two collections of short stories, and five novels.

www.ingramcontent.com/pod-product-compliance
Lightning Source LLC
LaVergne TN
LVHW041619070426
835507LV00008B/333